D0375637

ITALIAN FAMILY COOKING

WITH ILLUSTRATIONS BY

ITALIAN FAMILY COOKING

Edward Giobbi

Cham, Lisa and Gena Giobbi

 VINTAGE BOOKS   A DIVISION OF RANDOM HOUSE   NEW YORK

VINTAGE BOOKS EDITION, March 1978

Copyright © 1971 by Edward Giobbi
All rights reserved under International and Pan-American Copyright Conven-
tions. Published in the United States by Random House, Inc., New York, and
simultaneously in Canada by Random House of Canada Limited, Toronto.
Originally published by Random House, Inc., in May 1971.

Library of Congress Cataloging in Publication Data

Giobbi, Edward.
Italian family cooking.

1. Cookery, Italian. I. Title.
TX723.G48   1978   641.5'945   77-92629
ISBN 0-394-72564-6

Manufactured in the United States of America

This book is dedicated to

My Parents, who taught me
My Children, for their talent
My Friends, for their encouragement
My Wife, for her patience

INTRODUCTION

It has always seemed to me that the people who care most passionately about food are those who grew up in an atmosphere where food was more than something to satisfy hunger. Those who know from birth that the having of food is a miracle. And that eating—the taking of daily bread—is a communion, something to be pondered over, wondered at and thankful for. And it was into just such an atmosphere that Edward Giobbi was born in Waterbury, Connecticut, on July 18, 1926.

He was a child of the Depression and the son of Italian immigrants. His father, whom he idolized, eked out a living first in Pennsylvania coal mines and later in Connecticut brass mills. The family's clothes had patches, their shoes had holes and there were few, if any, amusements, at least not the kind that money could buy. But there was food, special food cooked with infinite care, and it was around this that talk turned and lives veered.

Some of the most memorable meals of my life have been taken in Ed's kitchen, one of the handsomest and best equipped in America. And always between the talk of art, there is the talk of food. He will tell you an anecdote about Tommaso, a fabled, wonderful gentleman whom I never met but about whom—and about whose appetite—volumes could be written.

"Tommaso," Ed begins, "was my father's closest friend. Like my father, he worked like hell to make ends meet. He was a bachelor—he couldn't get married because he sent all his money back to Italy to support his mother and sister. But he used to make out with the ladies. And my earliest recollection is going over to Tommaso's house with my sister to watch him eat. He didn't eat his spaghetti; he inhaled it. I could barely see over the top of the table, and to me Tommaso was a giant. We'd watch him twirl his spaghetti—two pounds at every meal—around and around on his plate; and then, when he ate it, to watch that rapture on his face!

"Tommaso never spoke a word of English in his life. He finally made enough money to go back to Italy to live in 1950, and I went to look him up in 1953. I didn't know his address, and no one I spoke to knew of any Tommaso Buzzelli. Finally I explained that he had come back from America three years ago, and then they said, 'Aha, you mean the American,' and they showed me where he lived. He was a great cook, still making his sauces, sometimes with fish, sometimes with meat, sometimes marinara, and eating two pounds of spaghetti a day. He never went to a doctor, never went to a dentist, and he died a few months ago at the age of eighty-six."

During Ed's childhood his father and Tommaso found ingenious ways to eat well. They gathered wild mushooms and canned them; they made seining nets and used them in the waters around New Haven to get whiting and other kinds of local fish. They would spear eels and gather blue crabs and black mussels, mussels by the bushel. "They'd stuff mussels and spend the afternoon eating them. And there was always a garden, a piece of land on top of a hill. My father grew everything and made his own wine. My father thought it was degrading not to have wine on the table." And so did Ed's maternal grandfather, affectionately known as Nonno, who lived in Centobuchi, a province of Ascoli Piceno, in the Marches. This grandfather had a reputation for drinking five or six quarts of wine a day; and once, when Ed was an art student in Florence, he and a friend challenged the old man to a wine-drinking bout.

"I remember that dinner," Ed recalls. "We had rabbit cooked in white wine with garlic and rosemary and also *verdura trovato,* which means found vegetables. Now, you'll never find *verdura trovato* in restaurants, only in Italian country homes where the women of the family go out for three or four hours to gather about twenty wild vegetables and herbs, which they cook with potatoes. That meal was fantastic, and with it we started that contest with Nonno. As I recall we drank twenty-five quarts of wine before calling it quits. When I woke up the next morning I couldn't see the ceiling. Never such a hangover. I went to Nonno's house and found him sitting under a fig tree with a glass of wine in his hand. He never looked better. My uncle said he'd gotten up at five in the morning and climbed the fig tree. He said the only way to eat figs was while sitting in the tree."

Ed is without question the finest and most enthusiastic nonprofessional cook I've ever met. He cares about cooking, passionately. The most impressive feat of his that I can recall took place one summer day in Provincetown when he bought a 165-pound tuna off the pier and got it back to his summer home to can.

"It was so fresh," he says, "the blood was still warm. I cut off the head and cleaned the fish and put it in the bathtub. I let the water run over it overnight and added about twenty pounds of salt to remove the blood. It took about thirty-five hours to clean, soak and can, but I got sixty-five pints of the best tuna packed in oil you ever ate." I can testify to that; I remember fantastic antipastos made not only with that tuna, but with Ed's roasted peppers and deep-fried stuffed olives, and followed by his incredibly good pasta with ricotta and marinara sauce and freshly baked bread, home-grown lettuce salads and Italian cheeses and homemade Italian cheese pie, plus coffee. And all of it with Ed's homemade wine, which may not be the equal of a white Burgundy or Rhine or Moselle, or even Soave or Orvieto. But it is made with muscatel grapes and is kindred in spirit and taste to the Muscat wines that I recall in Morocco.

Ed Giobbi, his wife and three beautiful children live on a rolling estate in Westchester County. His kitchen, which doubles as a dining area, has antique utensils, including a *girarrosto,* or spit, that was found on an old wagon in Florence, copper kettles and stirring devices—it is a nonpareil. There are wood chopping blocks, a professional range, an open fireplace and Giobbi paintings, for Ed is, by profession, a fine painter.

And beyond the windows, in the spirit of his forefathers, are the good things growing that will grace the Giobbi table —tomatoes to be canned and/or turned into sauces, lettuces, eggplant, scallions, corn, Savoy cabbage, asparagus, and Italian pole beans that are direct descendants of beans his father brought back from Italy one year. And among the herbs are thyme and oregano, rosemary and bay leaf, garlic, sage, hot pepper and flat-leaf parsley. And most important of all, dark-green leaves of basil for that sauce beloved of Genoese—and Ed's family and friends—*pesto*. What a way to live.

CRAIG CLAIBORNE

East Hampton, N. Y.

August 1970

CONTENTS

ITALIAN FAMILY COOKING

This book is really not mine alone, but is a Giobbi family cookbook. It includes the recipes of my mother and my father, my father's friend Tommaso, my aunts and uncles, a Sicilian butcher, the reluctant proprietress of a seashore restaurant in San Benedetto del Tronto, where part of my family lived and where my mother now lives. My Memphis, Tennessee, wife's variations of her mother-in-law's bread are here and the minestrone soup of a lady from Perugina my mother met on an Italian beach one day.

Some of the recipes I have included call for fine and therefore expensive veal and for lobsters and other costly ingredients. However, my great delight is to nourish my family and my friends on home-grown vegetables, chickens, ducks and rabbits out of my own yard, with spices from my herb garden and wine from the cellar dug on my land.

I now live with my wife and three children in Katonah, New York, where such a life is possible, but long before we came here, I took enormous pleasure in buying food cheaply and in cooking—as I still do.

Even when I was a child, I used to love to watch my mother cook. Of course I never tried to analyze why it fascinated me so—I just enjoyed it—but I now realize that it was the creative process of cooking that intrigued me so and also the fact that it was such a natural involvement for my mother.

My mother enjoyed cooking. It was not a chore for her but an experience to look forward to, in spite of the fact that she worked eight hours every day in a dress factory, shopped on her way home, and cooked after that long hard day of work. Her great joy was Saturdays, when she cooked all afternoon while she listened to the program from the Metropolitan Opera on the radio. She would usually find something to cook that required a lot of time, so that her entire Saturday afternoon was spent in the kitchen. I remember the Saturdays of my childhood for that combination of rich food odors and music.

Sundays I identify with the odors of pasta sauce and simmering chicken roasting in wine and rosemary, plus the sounds of the Italian-language program on the radio. My mother loved to make pasta while she listened to the Sunday Italian program.

When I grew up, I went to Boston to study art. I worked hard at art school—though everything I learned there I've had to unlearn—and I was very, very poor. I *had* to live on one dollar a day and I soon realized that if I was going to eat meals nutritious enough to keep me alive and well, I would have to cook them myself. If I were to survive as an artist, I would have to learn how to live the rest of my life on very little and that meant cooking nourishing food so that I would have the enormous physical energy it takes to paint.

I was confident then that I would not reach my peak as an artist before I was fifty and that if I were to end up with an illness—perhaps even a fatal illness—it would mean that, through abuse and neglect, I would have wasted whatever talent I had. I was convinced that I had a real talent and something important to say and that my own survival was important. Thus, my original involvement with food was the wish to survive, to nourish my health in order to develop my art.

In Boston I lived in an apartment I rented with several other students. It had a very small kitchen and we had an arrangement whereby I did all the cooking and they washed the dishes. My first attempts, though edible and cheap, were not very good, and when I would go home once a month to visit my family, I would bring back with me as many of my mother's recipes as I dared to try. Slowly but surely my cooking improved and my confidence grew. I learned to cook a number of very inexpensive dishes and in time I was able to feed *all of us* for less than a dollar a day.

My culinary adventures followed my art training. After three years in Boston I went to New York to study at the Art Students League. I spent my first month in New York in a dismal room in a flophouse. Again, I tried to aim for the dollar-a-day budget but it was impossible to do while eating in restaurants, and I was always hungry. I finally found a very small room—actually it was a kitchen closet—for five dollars a week in a Puerto Rican neighborhood of the upper West Side. There was only space for a small chest and a very small bed, and no more than two people could stand in the room at one time. However, linen service was included in the rent and, most important, so were kitchen privileges. I shared the kitchen with four middle-aged women, and from that moment on, the budget was no problem. I would cook beef kidneys, beef liver with peas, chicken wings with potatoes and rosemary, and other delicacies of that kind. When I could afford meat or fish I always cooked it with fresh vegetables that were in season. Pasta dishes, of course, were economical and, if prepared properly, they were also nourishing. I would cook pasta with fresh vegetables like peas and broccoli, or with a sauce made of a small amount of fish.

After that year in New York I went to stay with my family in Italy. I lived on a farm with my Uncle Attilio and Aunt Ada in a little town, Centobuchi, near the Adriatic Sea. I spent six wonderful months with them, painting and improving my Italian and enjoying the excellent food. I got more useful "art education" from my aunt than I had derived from years of art school, for I learned from her marvelous ways to survive as a painter. She taught me how an excellent soup or sauce could be made from bones. My aunt would make the most wonderful pasta sauce out of a beef bone, chicken feet, a chicken head and a piece of salt pork. I learned how to cook delicious, nourishing dinners with very little meat and lots of fresh vegetables, and I even learned how to make fresh vegetables like eggplant taste like meat.

I went to Florence to the Academy of Fine Arts and stayed in Italy for three and a half years. Then I returned to New York to live in a cold-water flat in Hell's Kitchen on the West Side. This time I had to wait almost a year before I was able to afford a small second-hand gas stove and a wheezy old refrigerator. In fact, most of the winter had passed before I was able to afford a kerosene stove to heat my studio.

In spite of my resolve, my early efforts at cooking had mixed results. In fact, the best meal I got while I was in New York was brought one day by my father from Connecticut, where my family lived, with all sorts of good food he and my mother had gathered up for me. (You can read that story in the Game section on page 128.) Again, my emphasis was on survival, though I learned to be a pretty good cook and cooking became a source of great pleasure to me. I had learned where to buy food very cheaply in New York. I used to buy my fruit and vegetables late Saturday evenings just before the stores closed and I would bargain for the produce that was still good but beginning to "turn." I did all my shopping in the Italian markets on Ninth Avenue between 35th Street and 40th Street. I would buy mussels or whiting for fifteen cents a pound and chickens for eighteen cents a pound. I could cook a three-course dinner for six for a dollar and twenty-five cents and, even today, by shopping in the same area, I can buy the ingredients and prepare the same meal for a dollar seventy-five to two dollars.

I would often ask the butcher, in those days, for a few bones "for my dog." Then, I would make the most exquisite soup with those bones, and I always had a pot steaming on the stove. It was several years before my butcher realized that I didn't have a dog. I would buy a beef kidney for fifteen cents and make it last for three meals, adding fresh peas one time, asparagus another, pasta still another time.

I enjoyed then—and still do—beating the system. Occasionally, now that my work is known, I get offers from colleges or art schools to come and teach painting. I turn these offers down because I am a full-time painter and I want to remain that, but if I ever did accept a teaching position, I would insist on having cooking facilities in the studio and I would tell my students that they must learn survival in class since painting is not something that can be taught. But, I would give them a survival course as an artist, not a home economist. Art students, when they leave the security and unreal atmosphere of the class, are totally unprepared for the existence that awaits them, and I would try to convince them that they owe it to their art to preserve their health and to eat well and nutritionally. What they need to know is how to adjust to the poverty and hardships that an artist must suffer in our society. Really, so many of the decent young people in America today are looking for a way to survive outside the supermarket system. Perhaps we have done them an injustice by not preparing them for their life's struggle.

Though I have lived all my life in an Italian environment—in my parents' home, for six years in Italy, in my own household now—I find that it is very difficult to take an Italian recipe and translate it into English because there is such a difference in the ingredients. Most of the recipes in this book are "family recipes," either those my own family has worked out, or those that we've got from friends, or from friendly butchers and fishermen, etc. For this reason, precision in measuring ingredients is not very important. When a recipe calls for stock, for example, you can generally use beef or chicken stock, depending on which you have in the kitchen. By the same token, though fresh or home-dried spices are much better than those packaged commercially, I realize that it is impossible for many home cooks to get anything else. Thus, when a recipe calls for a teaspoon of fresh basil, if you must use the dried commercial product, just cut the amount in half.

I have tested all the recipes in the book with ingredients available in the United States, but it is only because I knew what the food was supposed to taste like that I was able to do this. For example, Italians use salted anchovies, boned and rinsed. They almost never use the anchovies we get, which are packed in oil. Their tuna fish is better, it seems to me.

both in terms of quality and in the way it is packed. (In fact, I cannot understand why American tuna is such a sickly pasty-white color.) I can a tuna of 165 to 175 pounds in olive oil every year and it remains a delicate sienna and pink, the same color as the tuna fish that is available in Italy.

Cheeses are different in Italy, as are lamb and chicken, and the veal is, as almost everyone knows, of a uniquely superior quality (though American beef is much better than the Italian kind and we have a greater variety of fish that is much cheaper than Italians can get). In these recipes I have tried to reconcile these differences and I hope I have succeeded.

Cook the food in the book with a free hand, using your own creativity with the freshest ingredients you can get.

A word about the drawings. Though the reader will have to judge the quality of the recipes in this book, I am perfectly willing to comment on the art work. I will say simply that this is the best-illustrated Italian cookbook ever seen. The drawings were done by Cham, Lisa and Gena Giobbi, three wonderful artists who happen also to be my children. Cham was six years old, Lisa seven, and Gena nine, when they made the illustrations. Their drawings have the kind of direct, honest vision that I am interested in, both as a painter and a cook. Also, the children know my food so well that they worked both from their fresh memories as well as from life. For example, the black-and-white drawings of whitebait were done by Cham in Provincetown, on Cape Cod, where we have a summer place. Gena and I seined for the small delicious fish, and Lisa, Cham and my wife, Ellie, gathered the fish as we dragged the net in. I put some in a plate, and Cham drew them while they were still almost alive. Then I deep-fried them and we all ate them. All of the dishes illustrated here were known by the children, by color, form, and also by taste.

EDWARD GIOBBI

Katonah, New York

August 1970

ANTIPASTI

aṇṭipasṭi

The word *antipasto* means "before the pasta." This course is served with most complete Italian meals.

There are literally hundreds of combinations, hot and cold, fish, meats, vegetables. Antipasti can be arranged to make a beautiful presentation, with a combination of colors and forms that are artful and delicious. Improvise with what you have in the house or with foods that are in season. Of course, antipasti can also be made with very expensive ingredients and can get quite complicated, depending upon the kind of meal you're planning.

OLIVE OIL

Olive oil is used in many of the antipasti recipes, as well as throughout the book. It is the most misunderstood food in America. If a tin claims the oil is 100 percent virgin olive oil, Americans assume it is the best. Actually, there are many kinds of olives, varying from excellent to very poor, from which oil, 100 percent virgin or not, is made. The best olives, of course, produce the best oil.

My grandfather made his own olive oil, and when I

asked him why there was such a price discrepancy between one virgin oil and another he said it was a question of olives. He said the reason that cheaper oils go rancid is because of the worms in the olives. How true this is I do not know, but I do know that a fine olive oil will not go rancid. As a matter of fact, I have preserved fresh pesto in olive oil, unsealed and unrefrigerated, for over a year, and the oil has remained sweet and good.

In Italy most Italians use a darker, less refined olive oil. It has a strong wholesome quality and is usually used sparingly and raw, especially on vegetables. During the past five years tinned oils have become more popular in Italy too. During the Depression my mother would use the fine imported olive oils for medicine. We could not afford just to eat it.

CAPONATA ALLA SICILIANA
Caponata Sicilian Style

2 medium eggplant
¾ cup olive oil
1 cup chopped celery
2 medium onions, chopped
1 cup coarsely chopped tomato
¼ cup capers
4 tablespoons wine vinegar
1 tablespoon sugar
2 teaspoons pignoli nuts
Salt and freshly ground black pepper
1 can (7-ounce) tuna, packed in olive oil

Peel eggplant and cut into ¾-inch cubes. Pour olive oil into skillet. Add eggplant and cook over high heat, for 8 to 10 minutes, or until lightly browned. Mix often.

Remove eggplant with a slotted spoon but leave the oil in the skillet. Place celery on one side of skillet and onions on the other side. Lower heat, cover and simmer, stirring occasionally. When celery is tender, add tomatoes. Cover and continue to cook for 10 more minutes, mixing together onions, celery and tomatoes. After 10 minutes, add eggplant to the mixture.

Meanwhile, drain capers, soak them in cold water for 15 minutes, then drain again and blot with paper towels. In a separate pan, heat vinegar and sugar together. As soon as the mixture boils, add capers, pignoli nuts, salt and pepper to taste. Simmer for 1 minute, then add to the eggplant mixture and cook over a low heat, covered, for 5 minutes.

Cool, add tuna and mix well. Serves 8.

OLIVE RIPIENE
Stuffed Green Olives

½ cup cappelletti stuffing
24 very large green olives, pitted
1 egg
Salt and freshly ground black pepper
Bread crumbs
Corn or peanut oil

Prepare cappelletti stuffing according to directions on page 42. Pit olives by cutting flesh away from pit in a circular motion from end to end, so that you have one continuous strip of olive (like peeling an orange). Stuff each olive with about 1 teaspoon of stuffing. Mold olive strip back into its original shape. Repeat process with each olive.

Beat together egg and salt and pepper to taste. Dip olives in egg mixture, then roll in bread crumbs. Fry in deep hot oil until olives are lightly browned. Blot olives on paper towels and keep them hot. Serves 4 to 6.

PEPERONI ARROSTITI
Roasted Peppers

This is an excellent summer dish with broiled tomatoes, boiled meats, in sandwiches or in antipasto. It can stay in the refrigerator at least a week. Roasted peppers are a poor man's dish that Italian farmers eat all summer long.

6 large peppers, red or yellow*
2 tablespoons chopped parsley, Italian if possible
2 cloves garlic, peeled and sliced
2 tablespoons olive oil
Salt and freshly ground black pepper to taste

* Green peppers can also be used.

Place whole peppers directly on the grate over gas, flame or electric burner. Roast over low heat, turning peppers as soon as their skins begin to char. The skin of the pepper must blister, but the flesh must not burn. Roast until the entire pepper is blistered.

Stand peppers on end and set aside to cool. As soon as they are cool enough to handle, core, seed and peel off the skins. Cut the peppers into strips ½ inch wide.

Mix peppers with remaining ingredients and refrigerate. Discard garlic before serving. Serve at a little cooler than room temperature to 6 or 8.

POMODORI ALLA GRATICOLA
Broiled Tomatoes

This dish is excellent in antipasto or as a cold vegetable in summer. It is usually served with roasted peppers and will keep in the refrigerator for at least one week.

3 large tomatoes
2 to 3 garlic cloves, slivered
2 tablespoons olive oil
1 teaspoon fresh rosemary
Salt and freshly ground black pepper

Cut tomatoes in half, crosswise. Arrange halves in a broiling tray to fit snugly. Put two slivers of garlic onto each half. Sprinkle with olive oil, rosemary, salt and pepper to taste.

Broil under high heat for 10 minutes or until edges of the tomatoes begin to brown. Let tomatoes cool. Discard garlic slivers. Serve at room temperature with the pan drippings poured over the tomatoes. Serves 6.

SCAMPI E CARCIOFI ALLA SAN BENEDETESE
Shrimp and Artichoke Hearts San Benedetto Style

1 pound raw shrimp, in shell
1 can (15-ounce) artichoke hearts
Juice of 1 lemon
2 tablespoons olive oil
1 teaspoon finely chopped fresh mint or ½ teaspoon dried mint
1 teaspoon finely chopped parsley, Italian if possible
Salt and hot pepper or freshly ground black pepper to taste

Boil shrimp in a little water for 5 minutes. Shell, de-vein and cut into slices about ⅛ inch thick. Set shrimp aside.

Drain artichoke hearts and chop into pieces no coarser than rough bread crumbs. Mix well with shrimp and remaining ingredients. Serve chilled or at room temperature to 6 to 8.

INSALATA DI TONNO E PEPERONI ARROSTITI
Tuna and Roast Pepper Salad

2 large peppers (red, green or yellow)
1 can (7-ounce) tuna fish, packed in olive oil
2 tablespoons chopped parsley, Italian if possible
1 teaspoon fresh mint or ½ teaspoon dried mint
Salt and freshly ground black pepper to taste
Olive oil to moisten

Roast peppers as directed in recipe for Roasted Peppers (page 6). Trim, remove seeds and skins and cut into ½-inch strips.

Mix pepper with all ingredients. Allow to stand for 15 minutes. Serves 4.

Note: This salad is excellent with a wedge of provolone cheese and good Italian bread. You may use ½ red onion, coarsely chopped, instead of the roasted peppers.

TONNO CON FAGIOLI
Tuna with White Beans

1 can (7-ounce) tuna fish, packed in olive oil
1 can cannellini beans, drained, or 1 cup cooked dried beans*
1 small onion, finely chopped
1 tablespoon chopped parsley, Italian if possible
½ teaspoon dried oregano
1 tablespoon olive oil
Salt and freshly ground black pepper to taste

Break tuna into coarse pieces with a fork. Then mix all ingredients together and serve at room temperature to 4.

* Soaked overnight and cooked until tender.

VONGOLE RIPIENE
Stuffed Clams (or Mussels)

16 littleneck clams or mussels
½ cup bread crumbs
½ teaspoon dried oregano
1½ teaspoons finely chopped parsley, Italian if possible
2 tablespoons grated Parmesan or Romano cheese
3 tablespoons olive oil
4 tablespoons dry white wine
Salt and freshly ground black pepper to taste

Open clams, loosen each clam from its shell and save the liquid. Discard top shell. Place opened clams, now on half shell, on a baking sheet. Mix all remaining ingredients except 2 table-spoons of the wine and blend well. Sprinkle each with a generous amount of stuffing. Strain clam juice and sprinkle over stuffing. Pour remaining 2 tablespoons of wine on the bottom of the tray.

Broil clams under high heat until the bread crumbs begin to brown. Pour liquid from the bottom of the baking sheet over the clams and serve immediately. Serves 4 as an antipasto.
Note: This same stuffing is excellent for stuffed mussels and stuffed mushrooms. It also makes an excellent stuffing for fish.

minestre

Soups

Gene Giobbi

MINESTRA DI FAGIOLI E GRANOTURCO
Bean and Corn Soup

Whenever I make bean and corn soup, which was my grandfather's favorite, I remember an experience I had with him. Really, I can never forget it.

The first year I lived in Florence, as a student at the Academy of Fine Arts, I shared an apartment with a friend who was working on his Ph.D. in art history. During spring vacation I invited him to visit with me at my relatives' home in Centobuchi, in the Marches. When we arrived, we were invited to my grandfather's house for dinner and there we ate rabbit cooked in wine sauce and verdura trovato, *"found vegetables," gathered from the field that very afternoon. My friend Al, my grandfather and I sat around for most of the night drinking my grandfather's wine. It seemed to me, before we left, that the old man was beginning to feel the effects and when we went back to see how he was the next day he was quite embarrassed by the fact that two young Americans had outdrunk him. He explained that he'd eaten very little that day and that he had already consumed his daily five-liter quota of wine before we arrived. He invited us to come back soon for a return match but told me to let him know the day before so that he would have time to prepare himself for some serious drinking. My friend and I laughingly agreed to the challenge.*

We returned to Centobuchi a month or so later and we sent word to my grandfather that we'd come. He invited us to dinner the following evening and again we had rabbit in wine and verdura *trovato. Al and I ate a hearty meal to prepare ourselves for the drinking bout which was scheduled to follow dinner.*

When we had finished eating, Al, my uncle Attilio, my grandfather and I began. My uncle poured the wine and kept the supply flowing. We would salute each other before each drink and then swallow down the wine. This went on for several hours, until we had consumed, among the four of us, eight liters of wine. At that point my uncle dropped out, and we three champions continued. We drank and we drank and we drank. Eventually I had to force down each new glass, but when I looked across at Grandfather, he seemed to be enjoying every drop, almost inhaling the wine, with a knowing smile on his face. When the total count reached twenty-five liters, Al and I admitted defeat and called it quits. All that I remember after that is staggering down the dirt road at about two o'clock in the morning singing, "Che gelida manina," arm in arm with my friend, supported on either side by my uncle and my aunt.

I woke up with a terrible hangover and my first thought was, My God, my poor grandfather, that poor seventy-four-year-old man. Feeble and pale, Al and I rushed to Grandfather's house expecting to find him in a terrible state. As we came close to his house, we saw him sitting in the shade out front, sipping a glass of cool wine, looking fine. He said he had got out of bed at five o'clock that morning and had climbed the fig tree to eat figs. He added that a sensible man should always eat figs early in the morning in that particular tree.

Completely humiliated, I asked "the old man" how he was able to drink so much without feeling the effects. He told me that the secret was that he had eaten three large bowls of bean and corn soup for lunch the day before, and had consumed only two liters of wine, rather than his usual five.

Word spread about the village about la grande sbronza (*the great drunk*) *and we were looked upon with a certain reverence as the two Americans who al-*

most outdrank Martino Gasparetti. I've gone back to Centobuchi three times since my student days, and when I come, people still talk about the great drunk, though the number of bottles of wine consumed gradually rises as the years pass.

¼ cup cubed pork skin
1 tablespoon pork fat*
1 large can whole corn**
1¼ cup fresh shell beans
2 cups cold water
½ onion, chopped
2 tablespoons chopped tomatoes
Salt and freshly ground black pepper

Sauté pork skin in pork fat on oil. In a separate pot cook the remaining ingredients, except salt and pepper, for 15 minutes over a moderate heat. Add salt and pepper to taste, crisp pork skin and pork fat to bean-and-corn mixture. Simmer for ½ hour or until beans are tender, adding more water if necessary. Serves 4.

* Olive oil may be used instead of pork fat.
** Or use 2 cups fresh corn with ½ cup water.

MINESTRONE DI FAVE ALL'ABRUZZI
Dried Fava Bean Soup Abruzzi Style

2 cups fava beans*
2 slices salt pork, about 3 inches long by ¼ inch thick
2 cloves garlic
2 tablespoons chopped parsley
7 cups water
1 bay leaf
1 medium onion, chopped
Salt and freshly ground black pepper
½ cup of tubettini, ditalini or other small-cut pasta (optional)
Grated Parmesan cheese

* Soak fava beans in water to cover overnight.

Make what is called a *battuto* by chopping the salt pork, garlic and parsley together with a hot knife. Place *battuto* in soup pot and simmer over low heat until most of fat is rendered. In the meantime remove the tough outer skins from the soaked and drained fava beans and discard. Add water, bay leaf, onion, fava beans, salt and pepper to taste to the *battuto* in the soup pot. Bring to a boil, then lower heat. Cover and cook at a gentle boil for about 2 hours, stirring occasionally.

If pasta is desired, cook it in a separate pot until tender but firm to the taste, al dente. Drain and add to soup. Simmer for several minutes. Serve soup with grated Parmesan cheese. Serves 6.

MINESTRONE ALLA PERUGINA
Minestrone Perugina Style

My mother sent me this recipe last summer from Italy. I thought it might have some wonderful history, but it turned out that she got it from a woman from Perugina whom she met on the beach. An ordinary source, for an extraordinary soup.

6 cups water
1 cup fresh shell beans
1 cup fresh green beans, in ½-inch pieces
1 cup diced carrot
½ cup green peas
½ cup diced potato
½ cup coarsely chopped tomato
½ cup chopped onion
1 tablespoon chopped parsley
1 tablespoon chopped fresh basil or 1½ teaspoons dried basil
Salt and freshly ground black pepper to taste
3 cups chopped Swiss chard
3 tablespoons olive oil
Grated Parmesan cheese

In a large soup pot put all the ingredients except the Swiss chard, olive oil, and cheese. Cover and cook over a high heat until soup comes to a boil, then add the Swiss chard. Cover and simmer for one hour. Stir in the olive oil and serve soup with grated Parmesan cheese. Serves 6.

MINESTRONE ALLA GENOVESE
Minestrone Genoese Style

This is my favorite summer soup. A Genovese neighbor taught my mother how to make it many years ago. It is to be served cool, not hot, and it tastes better the day after it is cooked.

3 quarts water
1 cup fresh green beans, cut into ½-inch pieces
2 large carrots, diced
1 large stalk celery, diced
1½ cups fresh shell beans
1 small head cabbage, chopped
1 cup green peas
1 cup diced zucchini
1 cup diced potatoes
Salt and freshly ground black pepper
1 cup tubettini pasta
4 tablespoons pesto (Pesto #1, page 217)
Grated Parmesan cheese

Put the water and all the vegetables, except peas, zucchini and potatoes, in a large soup pot. Cover and simmer over low heat for about 1 hour.

In a separate pot, cover the peas with water and cook until almost tender. Add the peas and their liquid to the soup, along with the zucchini, potatoes, and salt and pepper to taste. Cook for 5 minutes, then add pasta and cook for about 7 minutes. Add the pesto and cook the soup several minutes longer. Serve at room temperature with grated Parmesan cheese to 12.

MINESTRONE DI CECI
Chick Pea Soup

1½ cups dried chick peas*
½ cup diced salt pork *or* 3 strips of bacon
1 large onion, chopped
2 whole cloves garlic
1 cup peeled and chopped fresh tomatoes or canned Italian tomatoes
½ tablespoon dried sweet basil
4 cups water
1 bay leaf
1 cup diced carrot
Salt and freshly ground black pepper to taste
1 cup tubettini, ditalini or other small-cut pasta
Grated Parmesan cheese

Soak dried chick peas overnight in water to cover. Drain.

Heat the salt pork or bacon in soup pot, stirring until rendered of fat. Add the onions and sauté, stirring, until wilted. Add remaining ingredients, except the pasta and cheese, and simmer 2 hours, stirring occasionally. Add the pasta and continue to simmer until pasta is tender but firm to the bite, al dente, about 9 minutes. Remove and discard garlic cloves. Serve soup in hot bowls, with grated Parmesan cheese, to 6 or 8.

* Or 1 can (20-ounce) chick peas.

ZUPPA DI CECI AL'OLIO
Chick Pea Soup with Olive Oil

1 can (20-ounce) chick peas
¾ cup water
1 clove garlic, chopped
1 teaspoon crushed rosemary
Salt and freshly ground black pepper to taste
2 tablespoons olive oil of excellent quality

Put all ingredients, except olive oil, into medium-sized pot. Simmer gently for 20 minutes. Add olive oil and cook, uncovered, for several minutes more. Turn off heat and allow to rest for 5 minutes. Serve warm to 3.

MINESTRONE DI LENTICCHIE
Lentil Soup

½ cup lentils
½ carrot, chopped
1 stalk celery, chopped
1 whole clove garlic
1 small onion, finely chopped
3 tablespoons chopped tomato
Pinch of oregano
1 slice salt pork, about 3 inches long and 1 inch wide
3 cups water
1 small potato, diced
1 teaspoon chopped parsley
Salt and freshly ground black pepper to taste
Grated Parmesan cheese

Put all ingredients except potato, parsley and cheese in soup pot. Cook gently for 1½ hours. Add potatoes and when they are tender, remove salt pork and garlic. Serve hot, sprinkled with parsley and grated cheese, to 4.

MINESTRONE DI LENTICCHIE CON ZAMPONE
Lentil Soup with Pig's Feet

2 pig's feet, split
2 onions, chopped
4 tablespoons olive oil
3 whole cloves garlic
1 cup lentils
1 cup chopped carrot
1 cup chopped tomato
1 cup chopped celery
1 tablespoon chopped fresh basil
5 cups water
Salt and freshly ground black pepper to taste
Grated Parmesan cheese

Sauté pig's feet and onions in oil in a soup pot. When onion wilts, add remaining ingredients, except cheese. Cover, and simmer over low heat for 2 hours. Skim off foam occasionally. Discard garlic. Remove pig's feet and break the meat into small pieces. Serve meat in soup, if you like, with grated Parmesan cheese, to 6. Also excellent with dried (soaked overnight) or canned cannellini beans.

MINESTRA DI PISELLI CON UOVA
Pea and Egg Soup

½ pound green peas, shelled
2½ cups water
½ onion, chopped
2 tablespoons olive oil
2 tablespoons coarsely chopped tomato
½ teaspoon dried oregano
2 large eggs
2 tablespoons grated Parmesan cheese
Salt and freshly ground black pepper

Place peas in soup pot with water and cook until almost tender. While peas are cooking, in a separate saucepan sauté onions in olive oil. When onion wilts, add tomato and oregano. Simmer 5 minutes, then add to peas and simmer 10 minutes more. Combine eggs, cheese, salt and pepper to taste in a bowl and mix well. Gradually add egg mixture to peas, stirring gently all the time, and simmer for several minutes more. Serve hot, with additional grated cheese, to 3 to 4.

ZUPPA DI PANE ALLA FIORENTINA
Bread Soup Florentine Style

This dish was a favorite of mine when I was a student in Florence. I didn't know how to make it until I finally got the recipe from a Florentine who was visiting a neighbor. The beans give the soup a wonderful rich base.

1 can of cannellini white beans*
1 bunch fresh broccoli
6 cups warm water
4 tablespoons chopped parsley, Italian if possible
1 cup chopped carrot
1 cup chopped celery
1 cup chopped onion
8 tablespoons olive oil
1 cup coarsely chopped tomato
6 slices of hard dark bread
Salt and freshly ground black pepper to taste
Parmesan cheese

* Or 2 cups dried beans, soaked overnight, and cooked in water until tender.

Drain beans and put them through a sieve or purée in a blender with a little of the liquid. Wash broccoli and cut into 1-inch pieces. Place beans and water in a soup pot, bring to a boil, then add broccoli. Cover, lower heat and boil gently for a few minutes.

In a separate pot, sauté parsley, carrots, celery and onion in olive oil. When vegetables are limp, add tomato and continue simmering for 5 minutes. Add mixture and salt and pepper to beans and broccoli, stir and simmer for 20 minutes more.

In the bottom of a serving bowl or terra-cotta pot, place slices of hard dark bread or hard French or Italian bread. Pour soup over bread and let stand for 5 to 10 minutes until bread falls apart. Serve soup hot with grated Parmesan cheese to 8.

MINESTRA DI RISO E PATATE
Rice and Potato Soup

½ cup chopped celery
¾ cup chopped tomato
1½ cups cubed potato
1 cup diced carrot
2 tablespoons olive oil or butter
1 cup chopped onion
6 cups water
1 teaspoon dried oregano
Salt and freshly ground black pepper
½ cup rice
Grated Parmesan or Romano cheese

Place all ingredients, except rice and cheese, in a large soup pot. Cover, and boil gently for 30 minutes.

Add rice, cover and simmer until rice is tender but firm to the bite, al dente. Season with salt and pepper to taste and serve with grated cheese to 6.

BRODO DI POLLO
Chicken Broth

1 3-pound chicken
4 quarts water
3 large carrots
2 large onions, each stuck with 2 cloves
3 stalks celery
2 bay leaves
2 tablespoons chopped fresh basil
1 good-sized beef bone
Salt and freshly ground black pepper to taste

Put all ingredients in large pot and simmer gently for 2½ to 3 hours, skimming the surface often. Remove chicken and set aside. Discard beef bone and vegetables. Chill the broth until it jells and remove fat from top, or if you are in a hurry you can remove most of the fat by straining the hot broth through a clean cloth. Soup is now ready to be used as stock or consommé. Remove and discard bones from chicken, put chicken meat back into the stock and serve immediately. Yields about 2½ quarts or 10 cups of stock.

BRODO DI GNOCCHETTI DI POLLO
Chicken Dumpling Soup

2 cups finely chopped boiled chicken
2 cups mashed potato, cooled
2 eggs, plus one yolk
2 tablespoons grated lemon rind
½ teaspoon nutmeg
Salt and freshly ground black pepper to taste
3 quarts chicken broth (see above)
¼ cup flour
Juice of ½ lemon
4 tablespoons grated Parmesan cheese

In a bowl, mix together all ingredients except broth, flour, lemon juice and grated cheese. Shape chicken mixture into 1-inch dumplings and roll them in flour.

Place broth in a soup pot, and bring to a boil. Add dumplings a few at a time. Cover, and cook at a gentle boil. After 5 minutes, add lemon juice, and cook 5 minutes more. Place 6 dumplings in each soup bowl with broth to cover. Serve with grated Parmesan cheese to 6.

Note: Dumplings may be served separately with butter and cheese.

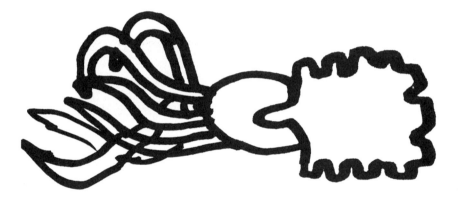

BRODO DI POLLO CON SCAROLE
Chicken and Escarole Soup

8 cups chicken broth (page 25)
1 cup rice
3 cups chopped escarole
Juice of ½ lemon
Salt and freshly ground black pepper
Grated Parmesan cheese

Bring broth to a slow boil and add rice and escarole. Lower heat and cover, stirring occasionally. After 5 minutes add lemon juice, salt and pepper to taste and cook until rice is tender but firm to the bite, al dente. Serve with grated Parmesan cheese to 6.

MINESTRA DI UOVA IN TRIPPA
Egg Soup, Tripe Style

1 large egg
1 tablespoon Parmesan cheese
¼ cup milk
1 tablespoon chopped parsley
Salt and freshly ground black pepper
1 tablespoon butter
4 cups hot chicken broth (page 25)

Mix together egg, cheese, milk, parsley, salt and pepper to taste and blend well. Heat butter in a small skillet, add egg mixture. Cover and cook over low heat until egg is firm. Remove it carefully and place on paper towel. When cool, cut in strips about ⅛ inch wide and 2 inches long. Place an equal amount of egg strips in each soup plate. Cover with hot chicken broth and serve with additional grated cheese to 3 or 4.

STRACCIATELLE ALLA ROMANA
Egg Drop Soup Roman Style

6 cups chicken broth (page 25)
2 cups chopped fresh spinach
2 eggs
3 tablespoons grated Parmesan cheese
Grated rind of 1 lemon
Salt and freshly ground black pepper
Juice of ½ lemon

Bring broth to a slow boil and add spinach. In a bowl blend thoroughly the eggs, cheese, lemon rind and salt and pepper to taste. Lower heat under the broth and as soon as it stops boiling add egg mixture. Turn up heat and stir. Add lemon juice and serve with additional grated Parmesan cheese to 4.

SCRIPPELLE 'MBUSSE
Crêpes in Broth

6 cups chicken broth (page 25)
4 large eggs
2 tablespoons milk
2 teaspoons flour
¼ teaspoon nutmeg
1 tablespoon chopped parsley
¾ cup grated Parmesan cheese
Salt to taste
1 thin slice salt pork

Prepare chicken broth; combine eggs, milk, flour, nutmeg, parsley and ¼ cup of the Parmesan cheese in a mixing bowl. Add salt to taste. Beat well with a wire whisk.

Heat a small skillet or crêpe pan, 7 inches in diameter, and rub the bottom with the salt pork. Add two tablespoons of the egg mixture; tilt the skillet so the mixture covers the bottom evenly. Return the skillet to medium heat and cook briefly until mixture is set. Remove the scrippelle or pancake and place on platter. Wipe the skillet with paper towels, and grease it after making each pancake. Continue making scrippelle until all batter is used. Sprinkle one scrippelle at a time with a teaspoonful of Parmesan cheese. Roll each scrippelle jelly-roll fashion, and place two or three of them in the bottom of hot soup plates. Bring chicken broth to boil and pour it over the scrippelle. Serve with grated Parmesan cheese to 4 to 6.

BRODO DI SCAROLE E POLPETTE
Escarole and Meatball Soup

This recipe was given to my mother by a friend who was a diabetic and insisted it was the only thing she could eat. The original recipe did not include any of the ingredients mixed with the meat.

1 pound lean ground chuck
1 cup bread crumbs
¾ cup grated Parmesan cheese
2 eggs, lightly beaten
1 tablespoon chopped parsley
Salt and freshly ground black pepper
2 quarts water
1 onion, chopped
1 carrot, chopped
2 stalks celery, cut in half
1 head escarole (about 1 pound), washed and chopped

In a bowl mix meat, bread crumbs, cheese, eggs, parsley and salt and pepper to taste. Form mixture into meatballs about ¾ inch in diameter. Set aside.

In a large soup pot place water, onion, carrot and celery in a pot. Bring water to a boil, then add escarole. Cook for 10 minutes. Add salt and pepper to taste and meatballs. Cook for ½ hour and discard celery. Serve soup with additional grated cheese to 6.

BRODO DI PESCE
Fish Soup

1½ pounds of any bony white-fleshed fish, with head on*
1 medium onion, chopped
3 tablespoons olive oil
½ cup sliced carrot
½ cup diced celery
2 bay leaves
¼ cup chopped tomato
2 quarts water
2 whole cloves garlic
Salt and freshly ground black pepper to taste
½ cup rice

    * Remove gills.

Sauté onion in oil in soup pot until soft. Add all ingredients, except rice. Cook gently, partially covered, for 1 hour, skimming occasionally. Remove fish and garlic. Add rice to soup and cook over medium heat, mixing occasionally. While rice is cooking, remove bones from fish. Return boned fish to pot and continue cooking until rice is tender but firm to the bite, al dente. Serves 8.

ZUPPA DI RISO CON COZZE
Rice Soup with Mussels

1½ pounds mussels, in shell
3 tablespoons olive oil
1 clove garlic, chopped
1 tablespoon chopped parsley, Italian if possible
1½ cups chopped tomato
½ cup rice
3 cups water
Salt and freshly ground black pepper

Scrub mussels well under running water with a hard brush and steam open. Remove mussels from shells and save the broth.

Place olive oil, garlic, parsley and mussels in a soup pot. Cook over high heat for several minutes, then lower heat and simmer for 10 minutes. Add tomatoes and salt and pepper to taste.

In the meantime, strain mussel broth and simmer it in a separate pot, uncovered, for 5 minutes. Add broth to tomato-and-mussel mixture and simmer for 20 minutes. In another pot, cook rice in 3 cups water until tender but firm to the bite, al dente. Drain rice and add to tomato-and-mussel broth. Simmer for several minutes. Serves 4.

ZUPPA DI CALAMARETTI
Squid Soup

½ pound squid
½ cup olive oil
¼ green pepper, chopped
1 whole clove garlic
½ cup tomato, seeded and chopped
1 teaspoon chopped fresh basil
1 teaspoon chopped parsley, Italian if possible
½ cup chopped carrot
1 cup green peas
1 cup chopped celery
3 cups water
1 small potato, diced
Salt and freshly ground black pepper
½ cup rice

Clean squid (see footnote, page 96); cut in ½-inch cubes. Sauté squid in olive oil with green pepper and garlic in a soup pot. When pepper is limp, add tomato, basil and parsley. Cover and simmer for ½ hour over gentle heat. Add carrot, peas, celery, 3 cups of the water, salt and pepper to taste. After 30 minutes, add potato. Continue to simmer until potato is tender. In another pot place rice and water. Cover tightly and cook over low heat until rice is tender but firm to the bite, al dente. Add to soup and cook together for several minutes. Serves 4.

PASTA
e RISOTTI
Pasta and Rice

Pasta

Whenever I think of pasta I think of my godfather, Tommaso, who returned to his native Abruzzi in Italy after he retired. He died a few months ago, at eighty-six. Tommaso was the most original eccentric I have ever known. He was my father's best friend, and all of my father's friends—and my father too—were eccentrics. The beauty of it was that they were not aware of this quality in themselves.

My father met Tommaso in the coal mines in Pennsylvania before the First World War. They worked in the mines together for over twelve years. Tommaso then went to Waterbury, Connecticut, to work in a brass-and-copper mill and my father joined him there. They worked in the mill together until they retired. Tommaso ate macaroni in one form or another every day. He bought his pasta imported from Italy in 25-pound wooden crates. When he finished with the crates, he would give them to me and I would make birdhouses out of them. Tommaso would eat two pounds of pasta at a sitting, yet he was never overweight and never went to a doctor or a dentist. (He had all his teeth when he died.) Tommaso boarded with his brother. He had never married because he sent all his earnings to his family in Italy. However, he did his own cooking and he made a superb meat sauce, a fish sauce and a marinara sauce. He also enjoyed *baccalà* (dried salted cod) with rape and olives. The recipe on page 104 is his. My mother always said that none of the Italian women in the neighborhood were able to duplicate Tommaso's sauce, but she would add that she thought that the reason might have something to do with the fact that Tommaso did not wash his pots as thoroughly as they washed theirs.

My earliest childhood recollections of Tommaso are of the days when my two sisters and I would say, "Let's go watch Tommaso eat." We would stand beside him as he sat with a huge mound of pasta in front of him and watch him expertly twirl the strands on a fork and eat the pasta with great musical gusto.

To me he was a giant and a man to be admired. Tommaso enjoyed our obvious admiration and awe and always performed—as only an Italian can.

The last time I saw him in this country was on Easter Sunday, 1958, just before he left for Italy. He was very elegant in a beautiful black derby and a finely tailored Prince Albert coat. He was smoking an Italian cigar, in a cigar holder he had made himself out of the thigh bone of a rabbit.

My father, after viewing Tommaso's splendor, turned to me and asked, "Can you guess how old Tommaso's coat is?" I answered that it looked new to me—Prince Albert coats were in vogue in 1958. My father laughed. "I was with Tommaso in Scranton, Pennsylvania, when he was fitted for the coat in 1922. He also bought the derby that day. It has lasted so long because Tommaso only wears the coat and hat twice a year—on Christmas and on Easter Sunday."

MOTHER GIOBBI'S RAVIOLI

This is a recipe that all children love, and it was my own favorite when I was young. However, we could afford ravioli only twice a year and we always had it on Christmas Day and on Easter Sunday. My three children also love it and it is because of them that I finally learned how to make pasta.

My mother had been staying with us for several

*months, and after she returned to Italy, the children con-
stantly teased me to make this homemade ravioli for
them. Though the recipe is very easy, it is a little messy
to deal with the dough and it takes time. Yet, the children love to make the ravioli and to seal the edges with
a fork.*

Pasta for Ravioli

3 cups flour (preferably unbleached)
4 eggs, at room temperature
Salt to taste
2 to 4 tablespoons cold water

Place the flour and salt together on a bread board or
counter top and make a well in the center. Break the eggs into
the well. Beat eggs with a fork, gradually working in part of the
flour. When half the flour is in, start working in the remaining
flour with hands. Continue to blend the eggs and flour, working
slowly in a circular motion. Scrape the board occasionally with a
pastry scraper or knife so that all the ingredients are thoroughly
mixed.

Gradually add approximately 2 tablespoons of warm water,
kneading constantly. Then add more as and if necessary. The
dough should be dry and not sticky, so add water gradually, by
dribs and drabs. If too sticky, add a little flour.

Sprinkle the surface lightly with flour so that the dough does
not stick to the surface, taking care not to add too much. The
dough must remain soft and pliable. Knead the dough in a rolling
motion, pushing it away from you with the heels of your hands.
Knead for 15 to 20 minutes, or until the dough is velvet-like and
smooth. Cut the pasta in half and roll each half into a ball. Flatten
the balls so that they resemble a cake of cheese. Rub each cake
with oil to prevent drying. Put each cake in a separate plastic
bag and let the dough rest at room temperature for at least 1 hour.
See instructions for rolling out pasta (page 38). Yield: pasta for
about 20 ravioli.

Ricotta Filling for Ravioli

2½ cups ricotta cheese
2 eggs, lightly beaten
¼ teaspoon freshly ground black pepper
¼ cup grated Parmesan cheese
3 tablespoons Romano cheese*

Mash all ingredients together with a fork until well blended. Do not add salt. Yield: 3 cups of filling.

* If not available, use all Parmesan cheese.

How to Cook Ravioli

1 recipe for ravioli pasta (page 37)
1 recipe for ricotta filling (see above)
1 recipe for meat sauce (page 215)
Grated Parmesan cheese

When you make the pasta for ravioli by hand there will be two batches of dough. Roll one batch at a time on a lightly floured board into a circle about 20 inches in diameter. Give dough quarter-turns while rolling it, keeping the board lightly floured. Fill and prepare one circle before rolling the second batch.

Start at the top of the circle and spoon about 30 separate tablespoonfuls of ricotta filling onto half the circle. Leave about 1½ inches of space between each spoonful of filling. Lightly flour the surface beneath the dough as you work. Fold the other half of the circle over to cover the little mounds of filling on the top half. With a ravioli cutter or a sharp knife, cut between each mound of ravioli. Press the edges of the ravioli with a fork to seal. When all ravioli are sealed transfer to a tray. Roll and fill the remaining batch of dough.

Bring 5 to 6 quarts of water to a boil on top of the stove and add 1½ tablespoons salt. When water is boiling furiously, add the ravioli, a few at a time, and cook for 2 to 3 minutes after the ravioli float to the surface of the water. Use a sieve to remove each one carefully. Let drain briefly, then place the ravioli on a flat serving dish. Add a little sauce and cheese to each layer as they are cooked. Serve as soon as possible and piping hot.

Chicken Filling for Ravioli

2 chicken breasts
Chicken broth or water to cover
1 carrot, scraped and quartered
1 rib celery, broken in half
1 onion
1 bay leaf
2 sprigs parsley
Salt and freshly ground black pepper
½ pound spinach
¼ cup grated Parmesan cheese
½ to ¾ teaspoon nutmeg
1 clove garlic, finely minced
1 egg, lightly beaten
4 to 6 tablespoons heavy cream

Place the chicken in a saucepan and add chicken broth or water to cover. Add the carrot, celery, onion, bay leaf, parsley, salt and pepper to taste, and simmer about 30 minutes or until chicken is tender. Let cool in the broth. Remove chicken, discard skin, bones and seasoning vegetables. Put the meat through a food grinder.

Rinse the spinach and drain it. Put it in a small saucepan with a heavy cover and cook, covered, until spinach wilts. Drain well and cool. When cool, press spinach to extract as much liquid as possible. Chop the spinach fine and add it to the chicken. Beat in remaining ingredients with a wooden spoon, adding just enough cream to make a firm filling. Do not add enough to make it soupy.

PASTA PROBLEMS

It seems to me that I have never seen a book on pasta that accurately describes the problems of the inexperienced cook who attempts to make her own pasta.

The dough is simple. Kneading the dough to the proper consistency is just work, but rolling the dough so that it is paper-thin with no holes in it is something else.

It is easy for Italians because they start to learn when they are children. (My mother began when she was eight.) It is almost impossible to roll dough properly the first time. The pasta is rolled with a combination of pressing the cup of the hand near the thumbs and stretching the pasta as it rolls over the rolling pin. The technique involves two movements at once. Too much pressure will tear the pasta. When the art of making your own pasta (after many failures) is achieved, nothing is more satisfying.

You can, of course, use the pasta machine. It is easy to manage and you can make good pasta with it. But nothing is as good as pasta rolled by hand. It is harder, thinner and lighter.

As for packaged pasta, the imported Italian brands, available in Italian stores, are by far the best. American pastas cannot compare with imported Italian pastas. Most American pastas taste like glue. All the reader has to do is try imported Italian pastas once and he will be convinced.

PASTA BY MACHINE

I've discovered that the best way to make pasta with the pasta machine is to use semolina instead of white flour. My second choice is unbleached flour.

Make the dough exactly as you would if you were to roll the pasta out by hand. After the dough has rested for about an hour, cut the ball into four sections. Dust each section liberally with flour and gently roll out with a floured rolling pin. The dough should be rolled to the thickness of the largest opening of your pasta machine. Then roll the dough through your machine according to the machine instructions. If you're making the pasta for ravioli, cappelletti, lasagne, or cannelloni, use it immediately. If the pasta is to be cut into fettuccine or used as noodles, it should be spread out on the floured board and allowed to dry for at least 1 hour after cutting. Turn it occasionally so that the pasta dries on both sides. The cooking time of homemade pasta is from 3 to 5 minutes.

CAPPELLETTI
Little Hats

This dish is a lot of work. The pasta must be used rapidly so that it does not dry out. I do not advise that you attempt to cook this alone. Get someone to help you make and stuff the cappelletti. My wife and children join me.

STUFFING

1 tablespoon salt pork
½ pound lean pork, cut into 1-inch cubes
½ pound tender lean chuck, cut into 1-inch cubes
½ pound chicken breasts, cut into 1-inch strips
1 tablespoon butter
½ medium onion, chopped
¼ cup dry white wine
¼ teaspoon tomato paste
2 tablespoons stock or water
Salt and freshly ground black pepper
¼ cup grated Parmesan cheese
¼ teaspoon nutmeg
1 teaspoon grated lemon rind
3 eggs, beaten

Chop salt pork with a hot knife, then sauté. When fat is rendered, add meats, chicken and butter. Cook over medium heat, uncovered, stirring often. When meat begins to brown, add onion. When onion wilts, add wine and cook, covered, for several minutes.

Remove cover and allow the wine to cook out. Then add tomato paste, stock or water, and salt and pepper to taste. Simmer, uncovered, for about 10 minutes. Remove meat and chicken. Then discard remaining ingredients. Grind meat mixture in a fine grinder. Place in a large bowl and mix well with Parmesan cheese, nutmeg, lemon rind and eggs to make the stuffing.

PASTA

Make a ravioli pasta with 4 eggs (page 37). Roll out the pasta as thin as possible. Cut out circles with a small glass about 1¼ to 1½ inches in diameter.

Place ½ teaspoon of stuffing in the center of each circle. Fold the pasta in half and press the edges to seal. Then fold and seal the pointed ends together to form little caps. Repeat the process until all the pasta is used. (Allow about 8 cappelletti per person if you serve them in broth, and about 1 dozen per person if served in sauce.)

Cook cappelletti in plenty of boiling water for 5 minutes. Drain and serve with meat sauce (page 215) or marinara sauce (page 214). To use in soup, boil the cappelletti in clear chicken or beef broth and serve with grated Parmesan cheese.

TAGLIATELLE * CON PISELLI
Tagliatelle with Peas

2 pounds green peas
1 clove garlic, chopped
1 tablespoon fresh chopped basil, or 1½ teaspoons dried basil
4 tablespoons butter
Juice of ½ lemon
Salt and freshly ground black pepper
1 pound tagliatelle, homemade or imported if possible
Grated Parmesan cheese

Cover peas with water and cook gently until tender. Drain and set aside. Sauté garlic and basil in butter. When garlic begins to brown, add peas, lemon juice and salt and pepper to taste. Cook 2 to 3 minutes. Discard garlic. Drop tagliatelle into a deep pan of boiling salted water. Cook until tender, but firm to the bite, al dente. Pour pea mixture over hot tagliatelle. Serve hot with grated Parmesan cheese to 4 to 6.

* Tagliatelle are egg noodles about ¼ inch wide.

TORTELLONI VERDI CON PESTO DI NOCE
Green Tortelloni with Walnut Pesto

PASTA

1½ cups unbleached flour*
½ teaspoon salt
2 eggs, lightly beaten
½ tablespoon olive oil

Pile flour in a bowl and make a well in the center. Put salt, eggs and olive oil in the well. Stir until ball is formed, then knead for 20 minutes until dough has smooth, elastic texture. Roll into a ball, rub with olive oil and place in a plastic bag for 1 hour.

SPINACH FILLING

1 cup finely chopped spinach
1 cup ricotta, drained
1 egg
Salt and freshly ground black pepper to taste
Dash of grated nutmeg
½ cup grated Parmesan cheese

Cook spinach and drain thoroughly. Mix spinach with all ingredients, except Parmesan cheese.

Roll out dough as thin as possible, about $\frac{1}{16}$ inch thick. You may do this either by hand or by machine. Cut out circles with a glass, about 3 inches in diameter. Place a scant teaspoon of the spinach mixture in the center of each circle of dough. Fold it in half and seal dough by pressing edges together. If necessary, wet edges to seal tightly. Turn ends up so that they touch and form a little hat (same as cappelletti). Boil in rapidly boiling salted water about 10 minutes. Drain, place in a warm bowl and pour walnut pesto over tortelloni. Serve immediately with grated Parmesan cheese. Makes 50 to 60 tortelloni.

* Pasta can also be made with semolina instead of flour.

WALNUT PESTO

½ cup walnuts
¼ cup pignoli nuts
½ teaspoon dried marjoram
½ cup grated Parmesan cheese
3 tablespoons olive oil
Dash of nutmeg
½ cup heavy cream
Salt and freshly ground black pepper

In a wooden bowl mash walnuts and pignoli together until they are a grainy texture, or work them in a blender at low speed. Add all remaining ingredients except cream. (Although this recipe doesn't call for it, ¼ cup ricotta cheese can be added if filling is too heavy.) Just before draining tortelloni, add cream to pesto. Season with salt and pepper to taste.

SPAGHETTINI CON CARCIOFI
Spaghettini with Artichokes

5 small artichokes (about 2 to 3 cups)
Juice of 1 lemon
4 tablespoons of olive oil, or half olive oil, half butter
2 cloves garlic, split
1 teaspoon dried oregano
1 cup chopped mushrooms
Salt and freshly ground black pepper
2 to 3 tablespoons broth
¾ pound spaghettini
2 tablespoons butter
Grated Parmesan cheese

Choose very small artichokes, no larger than lemons, and you will not have to worry about the chokes. Remove tough outer leaves and trim off tips. Cut each artichoke in half, then in quarters, then in eighths. Soak these wedges in cold water mixed with lemon juice for 1 hour. Drain artichokes and sauté in olive oil in covered skillet over medium heat for 5 minutes. Add garlic, oregano, mushrooms, salt and pepper to taste. Continue to simmer. As liquid cooks out, add stock or water and cook until artichokes are tender.

In the meantime, cook spaghettini until tender, but firm to the bite, al dente. Drain. Add butter, toss with artichokes and serve with grated Parmesan cheese. Serves 4 to 6.

SPAGHETTI AL PESTO
Spaghetti with Pesto

This recipe was given to me by the maître d' of the Leonardo da Vinci, a Genovese. I never tasted anything like it before but he insisted that spaghetti al pesto was genuine only when made with potatoes and string beans.

When I was in Genoa I checked his recipe, and it turned out to be one of the most popular ways to prepare spaghetti al pesto.

1 recipe for Pesto #1 (page 217)
1 pound spaghetti
Salt to taste
1 medium potato, cubed about ¼ inch square
¼ pound green beans, cut French style
1 tablespoon butter
Grated Sardo or Romano or Parmesan cheese

Bring a kettle of water to a boil, add salt and spaghetti. Add vegetables immediately and cook until spaghetti is tender but firm to the bite, al dente. Drain immediately into a colander and transfer spaghetti and vegetables onto a hot platter. Toss with the butter. Add pesto and mix quickly. Serve piping hot, with additional grated cheese, to 4.

SPAGHETTI ALLA CARBONARA
Spaghetti Carbonara

There are a number of good ways to cook this unusual dish, but this recipe given to me by an Italian painter seems to me the best.

¼ pound pancetta or lean bacon
2 medium onions, finely chopped
3 tablespoons olive oil
Salt and hot pepper to taste
5 tablespoons chopped parsley, Italian if possible
½ cup chopped prosciutto
½ pound diced Fontina or Fontinella cheese
1 pound spaghetti
4 beaten eggs
Grated Parmesan cheese

Cut pancetta or bacon into 1-inch pieces. Cook in a small skillet until crisp. Drain on paper towels and set aside.

Sauté onions in olive oil. When wilted, add all other ingredients except spaghetti, eggs and Parmesan cheese. (If Fontinella is used, add to sauce the last few minutes.) Cover, and simmer over low heat, stirring often, for 5 to 10 minutes.

Cook spaghetti in boiling salted water until tender, but firm to the bite, al dente. Drain, place in serving bowl, add eggs, and toss well. Add sauce and toss again. Serve immediately with grated Parmesan cheese to 6.

SPAGHETTI ALLA FORIANA
Spaghetti Forian Style

This is a Lenten specialty from the island of Ischia.

4 tablespoons olive oil
2 tablespoons finely chopped garlic
3 tablespoons finely chopped walnuts
3 tablespoons finely chopped pignoli (pine nuts)
1 teaspoon dried oregano
Salt and freshly ground black pepper to taste
4 tablespoons white raisins
½ pound spaghetti
Grated Romano or Sardo cheese
2 tablespoons butter

Heat oil in a wide skillet and add all ingredients except raisins, cheese, spaghetti and butter. Cook sauce for 3 to 4 minutes. Add raisins and cook 3 to 4 minutes longer over low heat.

In the meantime, cook spaghetti in boiling salted water until it is tender but firm to the bite, al dente. Drain. Toss spaghetti in skillet with sauce. Add butter and toss again for a minute or so. Serve immediately with grated cheese to 3 or 4.

SPAGHETTINI IN SALSA ABRUZZESE
Spaghettini in Abruzzese Sauce

¼ cup olive oil
1 cup finely chopped onion
½ pound cleaned, picked-over zucchini or yellow-squash blossoms
⅓ cup finely chopped parsley
1 teaspoon or more stem saffron, crumbled and diluted in a little warm water
2 tablespoons water
1¼ cups broth
Salt and freshly ground pepper
2 egg yolks
1 pound spaghettini, cooked according to taste
Grated Romano cheese

Heat the oil and add the onion. Cook, stirring, until wilted. Add the squash blossoms and parsley and stir. Meanwhile, combine the saffron and water and add this to the mixture. Cook briefly and add ¼ cup of broth.

Start cooking the spaghettini.

Put the sauce through a food mill and add the remaining broth. Simmer 5 minutes and add salt and pepper to taste. Remove the sauce from the heat, and working quickly, beat in the yolks. Do not reheat. Serve with hot, freshly cooked spaghettini and grated cheese. Yield: 6 servings.

SPAGHETTI ALLA MATRICIANA
Spaghetti Matriciana Style

This delightful sauce is often identified as a Roman specialty because of its popularity in Rome, but it comes originally from Abruzzi, at the time when Amatrice was part of Abruzzi. There are many variations of this dish and cooking times run from "just heating the tomatoes" to cooking them for 30 minutes. This recipe is my own favorite. Fresh, ripe tomatoes must be used.

4 cups fresh, ripe tomatoes
¼ cup chopped lean salt pork or bacon
1 medium onion, chopped
Salt and freshly ground black pepper or hot pepper
1 pound spaghetti
Grated Romano or Parmesan cheese

Drop tomatoes into boiling water. Quickly remove them and slip off their skins. Cut tomatoes into pieces and run through a food mill.

In the meantime, cook salt pork in a skillet until fat is rendered. Add onion and continue to simmer, uncovered, until onion is translucent. Add tomatoes, salt and pepper to taste. Simmer, uncovered, for 5 to 10 minutes.

Serve over drained spaghetti, cooked al dente, with grated cheese, to 6.

SPAGHETTI ALLA PUTTANESCA
Spaghetti, Whore Style

This recipe was created by Neapolitan prostitutes. The aroma is said to be so tempting that it attracts passers-by.

2 slices Italian bread, cut into ¼-inch cubes
5 tablespoons olive oil
1 medium onion, chopped
14 dried Italian or Greek black olives, pitted and sliced
2 tablespoons tomato paste
¾ cup warm water
½ teaspoon dried oregano
Salt and freshly ground black pepper
¾ pound spaghetti

Sauté the bread with a sprinkling of salt and pepper in 2 tablespoons olive oil until crisp. Set aside and keep warm.

Sauté onion and olives in remaining olive oil. Dissolve the tomato paste in warm water. When onion wilts, add tomato-paste mixture, oregano and salt and pepper to taste. Bring sauce to a boil, cover and lower heat. Simmer for 10 minutes, then set aside.

In the meantime, add spaghetti to boiling salted water. When spaghetti is tender but firm to the bite, al dente, drain and add it to the sauce in the skillet. Turn up heat, and cook, tossing for several minutes. Serve hot, topped with the bread cubes, to 4.

LINGUINE CON CALAMARETTI
Linguine with Squid

2 medium-sized stuffed squid (see page 96 for stuffing instructions)
¼ cup olive oil
1 clove garlic, sliced
1 tablespoon finely chopped parsley, Italian if possible
2 cups chopped, seeded tomatoes
1 teaspoon dried oregano
Salt and hot pepper to taste
¾ pound linguine

Sauté stuffed squid in olive oil. Add garlic and parsley. Cook over low heat, turning squid often and carefully so as not to puncture skin.

As squid begins to brown, add all remaining ingredients, except linguine. Simmer, uncovered, over low heat for 45 minutes.

Meanwhile, cook linguine in boiling salted water for 7 minutes. Drain and add to sauce in skillet. Continue cooking over low heat, right in the sauce and tossing constantly, until linguine is tender but firm to the bite, al dente. Serve hot, with slices of stuffed squid, to 4.

LINGUINE CON POLPETTE DI PESCE
Linguine with Fish Balls

2 1½-pound whiting, filleted (reserve heads, skin and bones)*
2 cloves garlic, finely chopped
2 tablespoons finely chopped parsley, Italian if possible
1 egg, lightly beaten
Salt and freshly ground black pepper
½ cup grated Parmesan cheese
1½ quarts peeled, seeded tomatoes, strained
½ cup olive oil
1 teaspoon dried basil
Hot pepper flakes
1 pound linguine

Chop fish fillets as finely as possible. Add half the garlic and half the parsley and continue chopping until well blended. Transfer mixture into a mixing bowl. Add egg, salt and pepper to taste and cheese. Mix well and shape mixture with hands into balls 1 to 1½ inches in diameter.

In a skillet, combine remaining garlic and parsley, tomatoes, oil, basil and hot pepper flakes to taste. Simmer, uncovered, for 10 minutes, then add reserved fish heads, skin and bones. Cook over high heat 5 minutes, lower the heat and simmer 10 minutes longer.

Add fish balls and simmer ½ hour. Remove and discard fish heads, skin and bones. Then remove fish balls, set aside and keep warm. Cook linguine 7 minutes in boiling water and drain immediately. Add to sauce and toss well. Cook over medium heat, tossing constantly, to desired degree of doneness. Pasta should be tender, but firm to the bite, al dente. Do not overcook. Serve piping hot with fish balls. Serves 6.

* If fresh whiting is not available, use fresh pike, haddock, cod or halibut.

LINGUINE CON VONGOLE
Linguine with Clams

18 fresh littleneck clams
4 tablespoons olive oil
2 large cloves garlic, sliced
2 cups chopped, seeded tomatoes
1½ tablespoons fresh basil, or 1 teaspoon dried basil
1½ tablespoons minced Italian parsley
1 teaspoon oregano
Salt and hot pepper to taste

Wash clams, then place in a pot and cook, covered, over low heat until clams begin to open. Remove flesh from shells. Save liquid and coarsely chop clams. Set aside.

In a wide skillet, brown garlic in olive oil and discard garlic before it burns. Add tomatoes, basil, parsley, oregano, salt and pepper to the skillet. Cover and simmer for about 20 minutes. Add clams and juices and continue to cook, covered, over moderate heat for 5 to 8 minutes.

In the meantime, cook linguine in boiling salted water for about 6 minutes. Drain thoroughly. Add linguine to sauce in skillet. Turn up heat and cook in sauce, tossing constantly, until sauce saturates pasta and pasta is done. Serve immediately on heated plates. Serves 4 to 6.

TOMMASO'S LINGUINE CON GRANCHI
Tommaso's Linguine with Blue Crab Sauce

2½ cups ripe tomatoes, skinned and seeded, or 1 can (2-
    pound, 3-ounce) Italian plum tomatoes, drained
⅓ cup olive oil, about
1 large sweet green pepper, finely chopped
3 tablespoons finely chopped parsley, Italian if possible
2 large cloves garlic, minced
2 tablespoons tomato paste
1 tablespoon dried oregano
Big pinch dried hot pepper
1 tablespoon fresh chopped basil, or 1 teaspoon dried basil
6 blue crabs*
Salt
1 pound linguine

Push tomatoes through a fine sieve or a mouli to purée them. Combine with all remaining ingredients except the crabs, salt and linguine in a large, deep skillet. Bring to a boil. Then add the crabs, partially cover and cook 1 hour over gentle heat. Add salt to taste.

Have ready a big pot (no less than 7 quarts) of boiling water. Just before adding the pasta, add 2 tablespoons of salt. Push the linguine down into the water gently, taking care not to break it, until it is submerged. Boil briskly until the pasta is tender, but firm to the bite, al dente. Drain at once. Pour immediately into a large heated bowl and cover with the sauce. Arrange the crabs around the perimeter. Serve at once to 4.

Variations: 2 live lobsters may be substituted for crabs in the sauce. Bring them to the table together with the pasta but serve them afterward. Or 2 pounds of scrubbed mussels in shells may be cooked in the sauce.

If sauce is too watery, cook the pasta partially in water, then drain and finish cooking in sauce, uncovered, tossing constantly until pasta is done.

* To clean blue crabs (note that they should be alive), turn crab upside down and hold claws against crab's torso with one hand. With the other hand pry with a dull knife into the area where the flap is. Force off the top of the shell and discard. Rinse and save bottom with claws.

LINGUINE CON ARAGOSTA
Lobster with Linguine

2 or 3 small live lobsters
2½ cups ripe tomatoes, skinned and seeded, or 1 can (2-pound, 3-ounce) plum tomatoes, drained
½ cup olive oil
½ cup finely chopped parsley
½ cup finely minced green pepper
2 cloves garlic, finely minced
3 tablespoons tomato paste
2 tablespoons chopped fresh basil or 1 tablespoon dried basil
½ teaspoon Italian red-pepper flakes, or to taste
1 teaspoon chopped fresh mint leaves or ½ teaspoon dried mint
Salt and freshly ground black pepper
1 pound linguine

To kill the lobsters, plunge a sharp knife between the body and tail shell—this cuts the spinal cord. Set aside.

Put the tomatoes through a sieve or a mouli to purée, and set aside. Pour the oil into a skillet large enough to hold the lobsters and add parsley, green pepper and garlic. Cook a minute or so, stirring, but do not brown. Stir in the tomato paste and the puréed tomatoes. Add the basil, pepper flakes, mint, salt and pepper to taste and the whole lobsters. Partly cover and simmer, stirring occasionally, for about 45 minutes. Turn the lobsters in the sauce occasionally.

Cook the linguine according to package directions while completing the recipe.

Remove the lobsters and continue simmering the sauce while they are being prepared. When the lobsters are cool enough to handle, break off the claws and crack them. Cut the tails crosswise into serving pieces. Drain the linguine and pour onto a hot platter. Cover with the sauce and add the lobsters. Or serve the linguine and sauce first and the hot lobster as a second course. Serves 4.

PERCIATELLI CON SARDE
Perciatelli With Fresh Sardines and Fennel Sauce

This pasta dish is made by southern Italians on the feast day of San Giovanni. Wild fennel is used and is available in Italian food shops, before the feast day. Domestic fennel greens will do, but they are not as tasty.

½ cup olive oil
1 pound fresh sardines
2 cups chopped fresh tomatoes or puréed or canned Italian plum tomatoes, drained
1 clove garlic, finely minced
2 tablespoons tomato paste
¼ cup warm water
1 tablespoon fresh or ½ tablespoon dried basil
1 teaspoon dried oregano
2 cups chopped fresh fennel greens*
Crushed hot red-pepper flakes to taste (optional)
Salt and freshly ground black pepper
1 pound perciatelli or spaghetti

Heat half the oil in a skillet and cook the sardines gently for about 10 minutes, turning them once. When they are cooked, split them in half and remove and discard the bones. Add remaining oil to the skillet, add sardine fillets and garlic. Simmer, stirring, for about 3 minutes. Add the tomatoes, mix tomato paste into the warm water and add to the skillet. Season with the basil, oregano, fennel greens, hot pepper flakes, salt and black pepper to taste. Cover skillet and simmer slowly about 45 minutes. If the sauce becomes too thick, thin it with a little water. Serve hot with perciatelli or spaghetti cooked according to package directions. Serves 4 to 6.

* Keep the white-bulb part to eat on another occasion.

PASTA CON VONGOLE AL BRANDY
Pasta with Clams and Brandy

I had an interesting time getting this recipe. Several years ago my wife and I stopped off to visit my relatives in San Benedetto del Tronto in Italy on our way home from a visit to Greece. Everyone was wonderful to us and I decided to reciprocate by taking twelve relatives out to dinner. My uncle suggested a restaurant which served only fish. It was run by the wife of a fisherman. She was an excellent cook and the fish served was caught that day.

We started with a shrimp and artichoke salad, then had the pasta with vongole and brandy. I could not understand how the proprietress managed to saturate a broad pasta with a light fish sauce. Fish sauces are usually very thin, which is why a thin flat pasta like linguini is usually used. In this particular case she used a very broad pasta to which the lovely sauce clung. I complimented the cook and asked her how she did it. "I won a gold medal in Milano for this recipe," she replied. "I wouldn't give it out."

I explained to her I was an American and curious, and she grudgingly told me a few things—that you have to put the uncooked pasta in the sauce and then cook it in a terra-cotta pot over a charcoal fire. I knew she must blanch the pasta first and then bake it in the sauce rather than put the pasta in the sauce uncooked, and everything else was easy to figure out. Though it sounds odd, at first, to cook pasta right in the sauce, this recipe works out beautifully.

Grilled prawns, cuttlefish and red mullet followed the pasta that afternoon in San Benedetto. A fritto misto followed that, and after that we had larger fish grilled. Salad, fruit and a wonderful wine from the area. It was truly a great dinner. Yet, I felt sad that my grandfather was no longer alive. He loved fish and he used to say,

"Dopo un buon pranzo ce sempre posto per due kili di pesce" (*After a good dinner there is always room for two kilos of fish*).

6 tablespoons olive oil
1 cup chopped green pepper
2 tablespoons finely chopped parsley, Italian if possible
2 cloves garlic, finely chopped
4 cups tomatoes, strained
1 tablespoon fresh chopped basil or 1 teaspoon dried basil
1 teaspoon oregano
Salt and hot pepper
1 dozen small fresh clams, in shell
1 pound short tubular pasta*
¾ pound fresh shrimp, shelled, de-veined and cut into ½-inch
   pieces
¼ cup brandy
2 tablespoons butter

Put olive oil, peppers, parsley, garlic, tomatoes, basil, oregano, salt and hot pepper to taste in a medium-sized saucepan. Cover, and cook gently for 20 minutes. Add clams, raise heat, and cook until clams open. As soon as clams open, remove them from the sauce. Continue cooking the sauce, covered, for 5 more minutes over moderate heat. Preheat oven to 450°.

Remove the clams from shells, discard shells and cut each clam into 2 or 3 pieces.

Bring 4 quarts of salted water to a boil. Add pasta, and stir with a wooden spoon. As soon as water comes back to a boil, drain pasta. Put drained pasta in a terra-cotta pot or baking dish. Add sauce, clams, shrimp, brandy and butter. Cover tightly and place in oven. Bake pasta, stirring often, until it is tender but firm to the bite, al dente. Serves 6.

Note: Sauce may be made ahead of time. Add pasta, cooked clams, shrimp, brandy, etc., about 15 minutes before serving.

* Such as penne or rigatoni, imported if possible.

PASTA CON RICOTTA
Pasta with Ricotta

2 pounds raw spinach
1 pound fresh ricotta cheese
3 eggs, lightly beaten
⅔ cup Parmesan cheese
⅓ cup chopped parsley
2 teaspoons salt
½ teaspoon freshly ground black pepper
1 recipe for marinara sauce (page 214)
1 pound tubular pasta*

Preheat oven to 375°.

Pick over the spinach, trim away and discard tough stems. Rinse the leaves well and drain. Cook the spinach, tightly covered, in the water that clings to the leaves, stirring as it cooks until leaves are wilted. Drain well in a colander. When the spinach is cool enough to handle, press it to remove most of the moisture. Chop the spinach.

Combine spinach, ricotta, eggs, cheese, parsley, salt, pepper and marinara sauce. Mix thoroughly and set aside.

Bring a large quantity of water to a boil and add the pasta. Cook, stirring rapidly for 2 minutes only, then drain the pasta in a colander. Add the pasta to the ricotta mixture. Pour the mixture into a baking dish and bake 25 to 30 minutes, or until the pasta is tender but firm to the bite, al dente. Do not overcook. Serve with more Parmesan cheese on the side to 6 to 8.

* Such as maccaroncelli, mostaccioli #84, elbow macaroni or penne, imported if possible.

PASTA CON BROCCOLI NERO
Pasta with Broccoli

I used to cook this recipe without adding the water when a Sicilian delicatessen owner said, "No, no, that's not the way to do it, you miss the point." Then he described how his mother made it. It is a delightful and unusual dish.

I make it with ordinary green broccoli, which Sicilians often call "black broccoli," as they call cauliflower "white broccoli." This recipe originally called for red broccoli, which is sometimes available in Italian markets.

1 bunch fresh broccoli
¾ cups tubular pasta, such as penne or ziti
2 tablespoons olive oil
Salt and freshly ground black pepper
Grated Parmesan cheese

Clean broccoli, cut off flowerets, and slice stalks into 2-inch pieces. Cook in boiling water until tender. Drain, but reserve 3 cups of the liquid in which the broccoli cooked.

In the meantime, cook pasta in 6 cups boiling salted water. Cook until tender but firm to the bite, al dente. Drain and toss pasta with broccoli. Add olive oil, salt and pepper to taste and the reserved broccoli water. Beat oil into water to blend. Pour 2 cups of liquid in each bowl, then add pasta and broccoli. Provide spoons for eating this dish, and serve hot in deep soup bowls with a generous amount of grated Parmesan cheese. Serves 6.
Note: It is essential to use good olive oil in this dish.

PASTA CON ZUCCHINI
Pasta with Zucchini

2 cups sliced zucchini
1 tablespoon olive oil
3 tablespoons butter
1 medium onion, chopped
1 cup zucchini flowers, cut up, optional (page 206)
2 tablespoons chopped parsley
Salt and freshly ground black pepper
1 pound pasta
Grated Parmesan cheese

Sauté zucchini in oil and 2 tablespoons of the butter over high heat. When it begins to brown, add onions, zucchini flowers, parsley, salt and pepper to taste. Lower heat and simmer for about 10 minutes. Cook any pasta you like until it is tender but firm to the bite, al dente. Add remaining 2 tablespoons of butter and toss well. Add zucchini mixture and toss well. Serve hot, with grated cheese, to 4 to 6.

RIGATONI CON CAVOLFIORE
Rigatoni with Cauliflower

6 medium onions, chopped
4 tablespoons olive oil
¼ cup pignoli
¼ cup white raisins
2 cans anchovies, drained and chopped
½ cup warm water
1½ tablespoons tomato paste
1 teaspoon dried oregano
1 teaspoon saffron diluted in 1 tablespoon of warm water
Salt and freshly ground black pepper
1 head cauliflower, cut into flowerets
1 pound rigatoni

Preheat oven to 350°. Sauté onions in olive oil until wilted, and add pignoli, white raisins, anchovies, warm water, tomato paste, oregano, saffron and salt and pepper to taste. Cover and simmer over low heat for 20 minutes.

In the meantime, boil cauliflower in salted water for 5 minutes. Drain and set aside. Cook rigatoni in boiling salted water for only 10 minutes. Drain, but save 1 cup of the water in which it cooked. Pasta will not be done at this point. In a casserole put a layer of pasta, then a layer of cauliflower, then a layer of sauce. Repeat the layers until all ingredients are used. Add the cup of reserved pasta water and cover tightly. Place casserole in oven and bake 20 minutes, or until pasta is tender but firm to the bite, al dente. Do not overcook. Serves 6.

PENNE, RIGATI O ZITI CON ASPARAGI E SCAMPI
Penne, Rigati or Ziti with Asparagus and Shrimp

1 pound asparagus
3 tablespoons olive oil
2 cups chopped tomatoes, fresh or canned
2 tablespoons chopped parsley, Italian if possible
1 clove garlic, chopped
½ pound fish heads or fish
Salt and hot red pepper
½ pound shelled fresh shrimp, cut into 1-inch pieces
1 tablespoon pesto (Pesto #1, page 217)
2 tablespoons butter
1 pound macaroni (penne, rigati or ziti)

Cut asparagus into 1-inch lengths and cut the thick stems in half. Sauté asparagus in olive oil until tender, then add tomatoes, parsley, garlic, fish heads or fish, salt and hot red pepper to taste. Cover and simmer over low heat for 15 minutes. Remove fish heads and bones with a slotted spoon. Add shrimp, pesto diluted in 2 tablespoons warm water and butter. Cover and simmer 8 to 10 minutes more.

Meanwhile, cook macaroni in boiling salted water. When tender but firm to the bite, al dente, drain. Pour shrimp and sauce on top of macaroni and serve immediately to 4 to 6.

PASTA CON PISELLI
Pasta with Peas

¼ cup cubed salt pork or 3 tablespoons butter
1 onion, chopped
1 clove garlic, minced
¾ cup fresh or canned tomatoes, peeled and chopped
½ teaspoon fresh or dried sweet basil
Salt and freshly ground black pepper
1½ cups shelled green peas
½ to ¾ pound spaghettini, vermicelli or quadretti
¾ cup grated Parmesan cheese

Cook pork in a casserole until browned and rendered of its fat. With a slotted spoon remove and discard pieces of pork. Or, if pork is not used, heat butter in casserole.

Add onion and garlic and sauté until onion wilts. Add tomatoes, basil, salt and pepper to taste and simmer briefly.

Meanwhile, place peas in a saucepan and add salted water barely to cover. Cover and simmer about 10 minutes, shaking saucepan occasionally. If young and tender fresh garden peas are used, do not cook them for the full 10 minutes, cook only until barely tender. When done, add peas and cooking liquid to tomato sauce. Simmer for about 5 minutes.

Break spaghettini or other pasta into 1½-inch lengths. There should be about 2 cups. Cook in 1½ quarts boiling water until pasta is tender, but firm to the bite, al dente.

Put pasta and cooking liquid into a hot serving dish. Add the sauce and mix. Serve piping hot, with grated cheese, to 6 to 8.

RISOTTO CON SUGO
Risotto with Sauce

3 tablespoons butter
1 cup rice, imported Arborio if possible
1 quart chicken stock
Salt and freshly ground black pepper
3 tablespoons meat sauce (page 215) or marinara sauce
   (page 214)
Grated Parmesan cheese

Heat butter in a deep pot. Add rice and cook, stirring constantly until rice takes on color. Add 1 cup broth, salt and pepper to taste and cook, uncovered, over moderate heat, stirring constantly. Add more stock as it is needed. When rice begins to soften, about 15 minutes later, add meat or marinara sauce, continuing to stir constantly. Rice should be tender, but firm to the bite, al dente. Sauce should be thick. Serve hot with grated cheese to 3 to 4.

Note: Green peas, freshly cooked, are excellent in this dish. Add them during last 5 minutes of cooking.

RISOTTO CON ROGNONE DI VITELLO
Risotto with Veal Kidneys

KIDNEYS

2 veal kidneys
3 tablespoons olive oil
1 large whole clove garlic
¾ ounce dried Italian mushrooms (soaked in warm water for
   20 minutes)
½ cup dry Marsala wine
½ teaspoon dried sage
1 teaspoon crushed rosemary
Salt and freshly ground black pepper
1 tablespoon tomato paste
2 tablespoons chicken broth

Cut kidneys in half lengthwise and remove the fat and white veins. Soak kidneys in cold salted water for ½ hour. Then cut them into 1-inch pieces, rinsing them well in cold water. Dry with paper towels and set aside.

Heat oil in a broad skillet. Add kidneys and cook over high heat, uncovered, stirring often. When kidneys begin to brown, add garlic, mushrooms, wine, sage, rosemary, salt and pepper to taste. Lower heat and simmer, covered, until the sauce thickens. Then add the tomato paste, diluted in chicken broth. Simmer for 5 minutes, discard the garlic clove and set aside.

RISOTTO

One medium onion, chopped
3 tablespoons butter
1 cup rice, imported Arborio if possible
4 cups chicken broth
Salt and freshly ground black pepper
Grated Parmesan cheese

Sauté onion in butter in a deep pot. When onion is limp, add rice and cook until rice begins to take on color, stirring often. Add 1 cup broth, salt and pepper to taste and continue cooking, uncovered and over moderate heat, stirring constantly. As broth is absorbed, add more, a little at a time, stirring all the while. After about 15 minutes, add the kidney mixture. Continue to stir constantly, using more broth as it is needed, until the rice is tender but firm to the bite, al dente. Serve with grated Parmesan cheese. Serves 4 generously.

MALFATTI
Dumplings

2 cups ricotta cheese
2 eggs, lightly beaten
2 cups cooked spinach
½ cup grated Parmesan cheese
¼ teaspoon cinnamon
3 tablespoons flour
4 tablespoons bread crumbs
Salt and freshly ground black pepper to taste
Butter

Prepare mixture just before cooking. Mix all ingredients except butter together thoroughly. Sprinkle a little flour on waxed paper and with floured hands form little ovals of the mixture about 1½ inches to 2 inches long, about ½ inch thick and 1½ inches wide. Use about 1 tablespoon of mixture to make 1 malfatto.

Bring 4 quarts of salted water to a violent boil, then lower heat. Add malfatti one at a time. When they rise to the surface of the water they are cooked. Remove malfatti with a slotted spoon and place on a warm serving platter.

When a layer of malfatti covers the bottom of the platter, dot the layer with a generous amount of butter and additional grated Parmesan cheese. Keep warm. Repeat the layers until all malfatti are used, adding butter and cheese to each layer. Serve immediately on hot plates to 4.

GNOCCHETTI DI POLLO CON SUGO
Chicken Gnocchi with Sauce

24 gnocchetti (see chicken dumplings, page 25)
2 quarts chicken broth (page 25)
1 pint marinara sauce (page 214)
2 tablespoons butter
Salt and freshly ground black pepper
Grated Parmesan cheese

Boil gnocchetti in broth for 10 minutes. Remove gnocchetti with a slotted spoon and save broth for another use.

Toss the gnocchetti in butter, salt and pepper to taste. Pour on sauce and serve with a generous amount of Parmesan cheese to 4.

GNOCCHI DI RICOTTA
Ricotta Dumplings

½ pound flour
1 pound ricotta
2 egg yolks
1 teaspoon salt
2 tablespoons grated Parmesan cheese
1 grated lemon rind

Place flour on board and make a well in the center, into which all ingredients are placed. Mix together and knead. Shape dough into a ball. Cut a small piece off the ball, roll out on a floured board until it becomes a long tubular roll like a snake. When roll is about ½ inch thick, cut into 2-inch lengths. Repeat process until all gnocchi dough is used up. Bring 3 quarts of water to a boil. Add gnocchi and boil for 3 minutes. Drain, and serve with grated Parmesan cheese and butter to 4.

GNOCCHI DI PATATE
Potato Dumplings

4 large Idaho potatoes, or other dry, mealy potato
1 teaspoon salt
1 large egg, beaten
2½ cups flour
2 cups meat sauce (page 215)
1 cup grated cheese (half Parmesan and half pecorino is even better)

Cook the potatoes with their skins on in boiling salted water until tender. Drain and when cool enough to handle, peel and work potatoes through a ricer or food mill. Spread the mashed potatoes on a flat surface and let cool to room temperature.

Meanwhile, bring 4 quarts of salted water to a boil. Add salt and the beaten egg to the potatoes. Sprinkle 2 cups of the flour over the potatoes and knead the mixture as for bread. When smooth and doughlike, set aside.

Lightly sprinkle a flat surface with flour from the remaining half cup. Cut a piece of "dough" from the potato mixture about the size of a 3-inch ball. Roll it on the board with your hands into a tubular roll about ½ inch thick. Then cut the roll into 1-inch lengths. Continue this process until all the mixture is used.

Drop the gnocchi into the boiling water and simmer about 5 minutes. Drain in a colander and immediately place the gnocchi on a hot serving dish. Add the meat sauce and cheese and mix gently with a wooden spoon. (Also excellent served with butter and cheese.) Serve immediately to 6.

INSALATE

Salads

Lisa Giobbi

SALADS

A good olive oil and wine vinegar or lemon juice are the basis of all good Italian green salads. Use fresh greens— not just iceberg lettuce, but chicory or escarole, endive, Bibb, rugola, radicchio, all of which are tasty rather than bland like the iceberg.

Many of the salads in this section can be used as the main course of a light meal rather than as a side dish.

BARBABIETOLE CON TONNO
Beets with Tuna

2 cups sliced boiled beets
1 small red onion, sliced
1 can (7-ounce) tuna, packed in olive oil
Juice of ½ lemon
1 tablespoon minced parsley, Italian if possible
Salt and freshly ground black pepper to taste

Mix all ingredients together (add more olive oil if desired), and serve at room temperature to 4.

INSALATA DI FAGIOLINI
Pole Bean Salad

1¼ pounds fresh pole beans*
1 clove garlic, split
3 tablespoons olive oil
1 tablespoon fresh minced mint
2 tablespoons minced parsley, Italian if possible
Juice of one lemon
Salt and freshly ground black pepper to taste

Snip off both ends of beans and cut them into 2-inch pieces. Cook beans and garlic in boiling water until tender. Do not overcook; beans should be firm. Drain and rinse in cold water. When beans are cool, mix them with remaining ingredients. Discard garlic. Serve at room temperature as a salad or cold vegetable to 6.

* Fresh green beans may be used.

INSALATA DI CAVOLFIORE
Cauliflower Salad

6 anchovies*
1 medium cauliflower
2 tablespoons olive oil
1 to 2 tablespoons wine vinegar
1 tablespoon minced parsley, Italian if possible
Salt and freshly ground black pepper to taste

Bone anchovies and wash them in cold water. Then drain and chop finely.

Break cauliflower into flowerets and cook in boiling water until tender but still firm. Do not overcook. Drain cauliflower.

Mix all ingredients together and let the salad stand for ½ to 1 hour before serving. Serve at room temperature to 4.

* Use anchovies preserved in salt, if available.

INSALATA MARCHIGIANA
Marchigiana Salad

This dish should be made only during the summer when ingredients are garden-fresh.

2 cups sliced green peppers, about 2 inches long and ½ inch wide
1 cup thinly sliced red onions
2 cups sliced firm tomatoes
2 tablespoons chopped fresh basil or 1 tablespoon dried basil
2 tablespoons wine vinegar
3 tablespoons olive oil *
Salt and freshly ground black pepper to taste

Mix all ingredients together and serve to 4 to 6.

  * The amount of olive oil used in all salad recipes depends on the quality of the oil and the taste of your family.

INSALATA D'ARANCIE E D'OLIVE
Orange and Olive Salad

Wash the skins of several oranges thoroughly. Cut in thin slices, *without* peeling. Rub a salad bowl with garlic. Add orange slices and a good handful of dried black olives, Italian or Greek. Sprinkle with a small amount of olive oil.

TONNO CON UOVA SODE
Tuna and Egg

1 can (7-ounce) tuna, packed in olive oil
2 hard-boiled eggs, sliced
2 tablespoons olive oil
1 tablespoon minced parsley, Italian if possible
Salt and freshly ground black pepper to taste

Mix all ingredients together (add more olive oil if desired), and serve at room temperature to 2.

INSALATA DI RISO
Rice Salad

1½ cups rice
1 jar (6-ounce) artichoke hearts, packed in olive oil
2 hard-boiled eggs, sliced
1 tablespoon capers, drained
4 tablespoons olive oil
1 firm tomato, diced
Juice of 1 lemon
Salt and freshly ground black pepper to taste

Cook rice until tender but firm to the bite, al dente. Drain and rinse in cold water.

Drain artichoke hearts and chop coarsely.

Mix all ingredients together. Then let the salad stand for 1 hour before serving. Serve at room temperature to 6 to 8.

Uova

Eggs

eGGS

Italians rarely have eggs for breakfast. Eggs are used as a main course, usually in the evening, when people generally eat their light meal of the day.

My own favorite dish when I was a child was eggs and fresh vegetables. It was a one-pot dish that my father had learned to make when he was working in Pennsylvania laying track for the railroad in 1906 and 1907. The men would get fresh eggs from a local farmer and find whatever vegetables they could and cook up a nourishing and delicious meal, which they called, in dialect, *ciambotta*. My father would make the dish just for the two of us because my sisters and my mother didn't like it. Between Pop and me we would consume a dozen eggs and a panful of vegetables.

When I was in the service I used to dream of that dish. (I also dreamed about hunting for wild mushrooms with my father.) As soon as I got out of the Army and returned home I told my father that that was what I wanted, and he prepared eggs and vegetables for me as my first meal home and I think that he was delighted that I wanted his special dish so badly. Luckily, my wife loves it too (somehow, she thinks it's an elegant dish) and we still eat it often.

FRITTATA CON BROCCOLI DI RAPE
Rape Omelet

1 cup cooked rape* (page 202)
4 eggs
Salt
3 tablespoons butter or olive oil, or a mixture of both

Chop the rape and set it aside.

Beat the eggs with a fork, as for scrambled eggs. Stir in the rape and add salt to taste.

Heat the oil or butter in a skillet and pour in the egg mixture. Cover, and cook over low heat until the eggs set. Do not stir. Before serving, fold like an omelet. Serves 2.

   * Spinach can be substituted for rape, but it is not as good.

UOVA CON ASPARAGI
Eggs with Asparagus

1 pound fresh asparagus
4 tablespoons olive oil, or half oil and half butter
1 medium onion, chopped
½ cup stock
½ cup grated Parmesan or Sardo cheese
1 teaspoon dried basil
Salt and freshly ground black pepper
6 eggs

Cut asparagus into pieces about 2 inches long. Split thick stems in half lengthwise and discard tough ends. Sauté asparagus in oil or butter in a skillet, over a medium flame. Turn often. When asparagus begins to brown, add onions. When onion wilts, add stock, turn up heat and simmer for 4 to 5 minutes. Then add grated cheese, basil, salt and pepper to taste. Cover and lower heat. Simmer for about 5 minutes or until sauce thickens, stirring often with a wooden spoon. Carefully drop eggs in the skillet on top of the asparagus, keeping the yolks intact. Cover, and cook until whites are set. Do not overcook. Sprinkle with more grated cheese. Serve hot to 3.

FEGATINI DI POLLO CON UOVA
Chicken Livers with Eggs

1½ cups chicken livers*
¼ cup olive oil
1 tablespoon butter
Salt and freshly ground black pepper
1 onion, thinly sliced
3 green peppers, cored, seeded and cut into strips
1 cup peeled, seeded, chopped tomatoes
1 teaspoon chopped parsley, Italian if possible
4 eggs

Cook the livers in 1 tablespoon each of olive oil and butter. Sprinkle with salt and pepper to taste and cook, stirring, until lightly browned. Do not overcook. Set aside.

In a skillet, cook the onions and peppers in the remaining oil, stirring occasionally. When peppers are limp, add tomatoes, parsley and salt and pepper to taste. Simmer 5 minutes, add the giblets and cook 10 minutes longer. Break the eggs carefully over the mixture, being careful not to break yolks. Cover, and simmer over low heat until egg whites are set. Do not overcook. Serves 4.

* Chicken gizzards, trimmed and cubed, may be substituted for some of the livers.

UOVA CON FUNGHI
Eggs with Mushrooms

The original recipe calls for wild mushrooms. I make the dish with large white puffball mushrooms which I find in my own field and it is excellent.

3 tablespoons butter
1 cup sliced mushrooms
½ medium onion, chopped
¼ cup dry white wine
1 tablespoon finely chopped parsley, Italian if possible
Salt and freshly ground black pepper to taste
4 eggs

Melt butter in a skillet and sauté the mushrooms and onions without a cover. When the edges of the mushrooms begin to brown, add all remaining ingredients except the eggs. Cover, and simmer over medium heat until the wine almost cooks away. Don't let the mixture get too dry.

Beat the eggs and add to the mushroom mixture. Stir often and cook just until eggs are firm. Do not overcook. Serves 2.

UOVA CON PATATE
Eggs with Potatoes

5 tablespoons olive oil, or half oil and half butter
3 cups thinly sliced potatoes
Salt and freshly ground black pepper
1 cup chopped onion
2 tablespoons chopped parsley, Italian if possible
2 cups roughly chopped zucchini flowers*
2 tablespoons grated Parmesan cheese
5 eggs, beaten with salt and pepper

Sauté potatoes in a skillet with 4 tablespoons of the olive oil. Cover, and simmer gently, stirring and turning potatoes with a spatula. When tender add onion, salt and pepper to taste. Cover, and continue cooking until onion wilts. Then add parsley and zucchini flowers. Cover and simmer for 5 minutes.

In the meantime, mix grated cheese in a bowl with the eggs. Add the mixture to potatoes, together with the remaining olive oil. Cover and cook until eggs are done, stirring often while they cook. Serve hot to 4 as dinner; to 6 as a vegetable.

* Don't worry if zucchini flowers are not available. The dish is good without them.

UOVA CON POMODORI E PEPERONI
Eggs with Tomatoes and Peppers

Any combination of vegetables may be used in this dish: zucchini, tomatoes and onions; or peas, tomatoes and onions; or parboiled cauliflower, tomatoes and onions. These are wonderful one-pot economy dishes that are nourishing, tasty and very easy to prepare.

1 large green pepper
2 tablespoons olive oil or butter
1 large onion, sliced
½ cup coarsely chopped tomato
1 tablespoon fresh basil or 1 teaspoon dried basil
6 eggs
Salt and freshly ground black pepper
Grated Parmesan cheese

Cut pepper into ½-inch slices. In a skillet simmer oil, pepper and onion for 3 to 4 minutes. Add tomato and basil. Cover and simmer over low heat until pepper is tender, about 15 minutes. Drop whole eggs into the skillet, being careful not to break yolks. Add salt and pepper to taste; cover, and poach eggs over gentle heat until whites are cooked to desired doneness. Serve with grated Parmesan cheese and French or Italian bread to 3.

SALSICCIE CON UOVA
Sausages and Eggs

4 links sweet Italian sausages
6 eggs
1 tablespoon chopped parsley, Italian if possible
Salt and freshly ground black pepper
2 tablespoons olive oil

Put sausages in a skillet and cook them, uncovered, over low heat, turning often. As sausages begin to brown, prick a few holes into each one to allow excess fat to escape. After about 15 minutes, when sausages are cooked, remove them from skillet; drain, and cut into ½-inch slices.

Beat eggs and mix them with sausages, parsley, salt and pepper to taste. Put olive oil in a skillet and add the egg-and-sausage mixture. Cover and cook over low heat, stirring occasionally, until eggs are firm. Serve hot to 4.

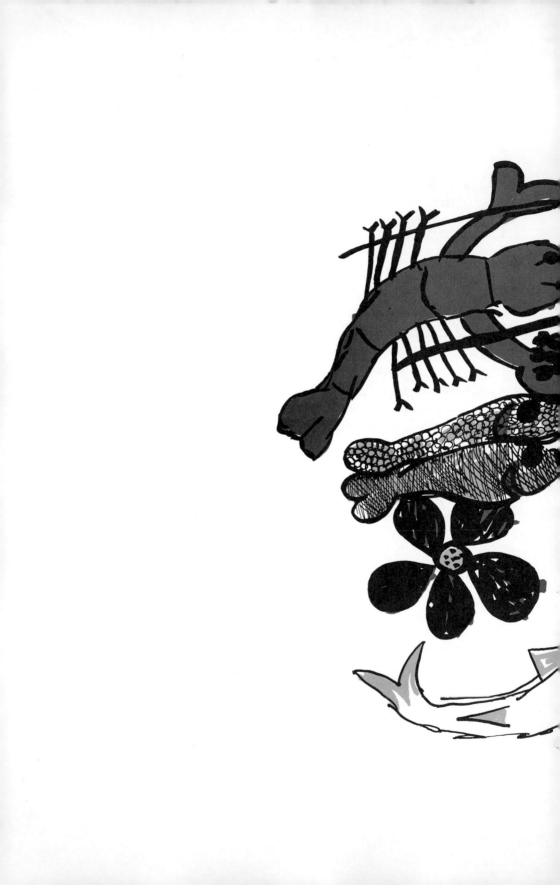

Pesci

Fish

gena giobbi

About

ℱISH

I think of the Depression when I think of fish. During the Depression, Tommaso and my father made a seining net about 20 feet long and 5 feet wide. The wooden floats around the edge we carved by hand. Tommaso, who was a fisherman in Italy before he migrated to America, wove the net by hand. It was a beautiful thing that took four to six strong men to haul in.

They used to go seining near New Haven, which is about seventeen miles from Waterbury, and they would all chip in a dime apiece to buy enough gas to get there. Tommaso, who was the best swimmer, was the anchor man and always the farthest out. He wore his black derby hat when he went into the water to keep the sun out of his eyes, and his Italian cigar in his holder (made from the thigh bone of a rabbit) was always clamped between his teeth. After August, Tommaso went into the water in his black woolen pants and a woolen shirt.

Whatever their costumes, the fishermen always harvested large quantities of fish, from whitebait to bluefish. No one had a refrigerator in those days, so when they got home, the fish would be distributed among the families, and everyone in the neighborhood ate well for days.

CHRISTMAS EVE
DINNER

In many parts of Italy, Christmas Eve dinner is the most exciting meal of the year. For devout Catholics Christmas Eve is a fast day, and the tradition calls for eating only fish. This is why the best selection of fish of the year will be found in Italian fish markets a few days before Christmas, and especially on Christmas Eve.

In our home on Christmas Eve, we would have seven different fish cooked seven different ways, representing the seven sacraments. It was a great meal, as this example shows:

> Baccalà with Rape
> Stuffed Mussels
> Linguini with Lobster
> Fritto Misto with Whitebait, Squid, Whiting, Smelt and
>> Shrimp
> Stuffed Cuttlefish with Tomatoes and Peas (cuttlefish are
>> frozen and flown from Spain and are excellent; squid
>> will do if cuttlefish are not available)
> Broiled Fish, usually mackerel
> Whiting in a White Sauce

We always had rape, broccoli, and stuffed artichokes. We would taste a little of everything, wash it down with my father's best wine, saved for Christmas. Christmas Eve dinner was a joyful time. How better to celebrate such a day than to enjoy the fruits of the earth in so creative a form?

PESCE SPADA AI FERRI
Broiled Swordfish

A 2-pound slice of fresh swordfish cut about 1 inch thick
1 teaspoon chopped mint
Juice of 1 lemon
2 tablespoons chopped parsley, Italian if possible
1 clove garlic, sliced
2 tablespoons olive oil
Salt and freshly ground black pepper to taste

Mix all ingredients, except fish, in a large bowl. Add fish and marinate it in this mixture* for 30 to 45 minutes. Remove from marinade and broil fish under a high heat, basting often with marinade. Turn fish over when lightly browned. Be careful not to overcook. (A piece 1 inch thick will cook in about 8 minutes.) Excellent with green peas cooked with prosciutto (page 199). Serves 4.

> * This marinade may be used for broiling or basting any large fish. It is especially good with whiting, striped sea bass, or mackerel.

MERLUZZI IN BIANCO
Whiting in a White Sauce

2 large whiting, about 3 pounds
2 tablespoons chopped parsley, Italian if possible
2 tablespoons olive oil
2 tablespoons butter
2 cloves garlic, chopped
½ cup water
Salt and hot or freshly ground black pepper to taste
Lemon wedges

Clean whiting thoroughly, leaving heads on. Place remaining ingredients into a pot in which the fish will fit tightly. Bring mixture to a boil and lower heat to medium. Place fish in pot, cover and simmer until cooked, about 7 to 10 minutes. Take fish from pan and remove bones and skin. Pour the liquid from the pot over it. Place fish on serving dish and serve with lemon wedges. Excellent with rice, or plain as a delicate first course. Serves 4.

MERLUZZI CON ASPARAGI
Baked Whiting with Fresh Asparagus

2 large whiting, about 3 pounds
2 garlic cloves, sliced
1 tablespoon chopped mint
Salt and freshly ground black pepper
1 pound fresh asparagus
1 tablespoon chopped sweet basil
Juice of 1 lemon
4 tablespoons olive oil
Lemon wedges

Preheat oven to 450°. Clean whiting thoroughly, leaving heads on. Place garlic, half the mint, salt and pepper to taste in cavities of fish. Arrange fish in baking tray. Place whole asparagus beside them.

Sprinkle fish and asparagus with remaining mint, sweet basil, salt, pepper, lemon juice and olive oil. Bake the fish and asparagus, uncovered, for 12 to 15 minutes, or until tender when tested with a fork. Baste frequently. Add more lemon juice, if necessary. Serve, with lemon wedges, to 2.

Note: If you like potatoes, boil them until almost tender, then slice, then bake with the fish and asparagus.

MERLUZZI CON POMODORI E PEPERONI
Whiting with Tomatoes and Peppers

4 small whiting, about 3 pounds
4 tablespoons olive oil
2 cups chopped fresh green or red peppers
1 cup chopped onion
1 cup fresh or canned tomatoes, chopped
2 tablespoons chopped parsley, Italian if possible
1 tablespoon dried basil, or 6 fresh basil leaves, chopped
Salt and freshly ground black pepper

Preheat the broiler. Clean whiting thoroughly, leaving heads and tails on. Heat the oil in a saucepan, add the peppers and onions and cook until onion is translucent. Add the tomatoes, parsley, basil, salt and pepper to taste. Simmer until the peppers are tender. Pour the sauce into an oven-proof baking dish large enough to hold the fish.

Brush the fish lightly on all sides with oil and arrange them on top of the tomato sauce. Place under the broiler and broil under high heat until fish is tender and cooked through, about 7 to 10 minutes. It is not necessary to turn them. Serve with hot cooked rice to 4.

Note: Any white-fleshed fish is excellent for this dish.

SCAMPI CON ASPARAGI
Shrimp with Asparagus

1 pound raw shrimp
1 pound fresh asparagus
3 tablespoons olive oil
3 tablespoons butter
1 cup chopped celery
1 half-ripe tomato, diced
½ cup chopped parsley, Italian if possible
1 teaspoon fresh chopped mint or ½ teaspoon dried mint
Juice of ½ lemon
Salt and freshly ground black pepper

Shell and de-vein shrimp. Cut asparagus into 1-inch pieces, splitting the thick stalks and discarding all tough ends. Heat oil and butter in a wide skillet. Add asparagus, celery, tomato and parsley. Cook over high flame until celery is tender, mixing often. Add shrimp, mint, lemon juice, salt and pepper to taste. Toss, and cook shrimp about 5 minutes—do not overcook. Excellent with rice. Serve hot to 6.

SCAMPI AL PESTO
Shrimp with Pesto

1 pound raw shrimp
2 tablespoons olive oil
2 tablespoons butter
Juice of 1 lemon
Salt and freshly ground black pepper
3 tablespoons pesto (see Pesto #3, page 218)

Shell and de-vein shrimp.
Heat oil and butter in a skillet. When oil is hot, add shrimp. Cook, tossing frequently until shrimp turn color. Add lemon juice and salt and pepper to taste. Continue cooking and tossing for about 5 minutes. Add pesto, toss and cook for several minutes more. Serve hot with salad or light green vegetables to 4.

SCAMPI AL FRESCO
Shrimp al Fresco

1 pound raw shrimp
2 tablespoons olive oil
2 tablespoons butter
3 tablespoons chopped parsley, Italian if possible
2 cloves garlic, chopped
1 teaspoon fresh mint or pinch of dried mint
Salt and freshly ground black pepper to taste
Juice of 1 lemon

Shell and de-vein shrimp.

Heat oil and butter in skillet. When oil is hot, add shrimp and cook over high heat, turning constantly. When shrimp turns color, add the remaining ingredients except lemon juice. When garlic begins to brown, add the lemon juice and continue cooking for 3 to 4 minutes, stirring occasionally. Serve hot for lunch with salad or a light vegetable, or as a first course at dinner. Serves 4.

SCAMPI E CALAMARETTI IN SPIEDINI
Shrimp and Squid on a Skewer

4 medium-sized squid, cleaned and cut into 1½-inch strips
½ pound shrimp, shelled and de-veined
2 tablespoons olive oil
½ cup bread crumbs
1 tablespoon chopped Italian parsley
Salt and freshly ground black pepper to taste

Mix squid and shrimp together in a bowl with olive oil. Then add rest of ingredients. Mix well.

Wrap a piece of squid around a shrimp, then stick onto a skewer. Repeat this process until skewer is full.

Broil over hot coals or under high heat until a light-golden color. Serve immediately with lemon wedges. Serves 4 as a first course, 2 as a main course.

GRANCHI
Soft-Shell Crabs

5 soft-shell crabs (live)
2 tablespoons olive oil
2 tablespoons butter
2 tablespoons chopped fresh basil or 1 tablespoon dried basil
2 tablespoons chopped parsley
1 teaspoon chopped garlic
Salt and freshly ground black pepper
¼ cup dry white wine

To clean live soft-shell crabs, lift end flaps and remove gills. Snip off front of crab where eyes protrude. Turn crab over, remove flap and wash. Crab is now ready to cook.

Heat oil and butter in a large skillet. Add cleaned crabs and cook, uncovered, over high heat for 3 to 5 minutes. Turn crabs over and cook several minutes more. Add basil, parsley, garlic, salt and pepper to taste. As soon as the garlic discolors (do not burn), add wine. Lower heat and simmer for several minutes. Serve hot to 5 as a first course.

COZZI CON VINO
Mussels with Wine

During the Depression my father and Tommaso and their friends often gathered mussels and I was always taken with them when they went to gather the shellfish. It still amazes me to know that people were hungry in Connecticut during the Depression—very few ate the food that was lying about so abundantly. The men of our community would gather bushels of mussels, and the Italian women in the neighborhood would make trays and trays of stuffed mussels (page 11), spaghetti with mussels, mussel stew, etc.

5 pounds mussels
¼ cup chopped scallion
¼ cup olive oil
¼ cup chopped parsley, Italian if possible
2 tablespoons chopped fresh basil or 1 tablespoon dried basil
1 tablespoon chopped garlic
¼ cup chopped green pepper
1 tablespoon oregano
½ cup dry white wine
1 tablespoon chopped fresh mint or 1 teaspoon dried mint
Salt and hot red pepper to taste

Scrub mussels well under running water with a hard brush. Put all other ingredients into a large kettle. When the mixture comes to a boil, add mussels. Cover, and cook over high heat until mussels open, about 8 minutes.

Drain liquid from mussels and serve in separate bowls. As you cat, dip mussels in liquid, as you would steamer clams in broth. Serve with French or Italian bread to dip in the liquid or sauce. Serves 4 to 6.

CALAMARETTI CON PISELLI
Stuffed Squid with Peas

4 whole squid, each about 7 inches long, cleaned at fish
    market*
2 tablespoons finely chopped parsley
1 clove garlic, finely minced
10 tablespoons olive oil
¾ cup bread crumbs
⅓ cup finely chopped green pepper
¼ teaspoon hot crushed red pepper (optional)
Salt
1 teaspoon dried rosemary
¼ cup fresh or frozen peas

Preheat oven to 450°.

Combine the parsley, garlic, 6 tablespoons of the oil, 2 tablespoons water, bread crumbs, green pepper, hot pepper and salt
to taste. Blend well and stuff the squid with the mixture. Sew
each opening to close it and stitch tentacles to the body with
string, so that squid is back in its original shape. Place the stuffed
squid in a deep baking dish. Sprinkle with remaining oil and
salt. Bake 10 minutes and sprinkle with rosemary. Reduce oven
heat to 350° and bake 10 minutes longer. Add the peas and 4
tablespoons water and bake an additional 10 minutes. Serve hot
with rice. Serves 4 or 6, depending on the size of the squid.

    * Many fish stores will clean squid for you, but to do it yourself,
first remove the head, then pull out the insides carefully, keeping the
tubelike body intact for stuffing. Remove and discard the outside skin.
Wash the squid well. Cut off the tentacles just below the eyes and set
aside.

FRITTO MISTO #1
Mixed Fry #1

3 small whiting, cut in half
½ pound smelt
1 pound squid, cleaned at fish market
½ pound raw shrimp
2 cups flour, about
Corn or peanut oil
Salt

Wash all fish, leaving heads on, and blot with paper towels. Cut squid into ½-inch strips. Shell and de-vein shrimp. Spread flour on a piece of waxed paper. Dust fish in flour.

Fill deep skillet half full with oil and heat over high heat. When oil seems hot, test by flicking a little flour into it—if oil boils violently, it is ready. Add fish, squid and shrimp, one piece at a time, being careful not to spill or splatter oil. When seafood is lightly browned, turn and cook other side. Do not overcook.

Remove seafood from pan, place on dish covered with paper towels and add a layer of towels on top of cooked seafood. Repeat process until all is cooked and on the plate. Remove towels, being careful not to break fish. Sprinkle with salt to taste. Serve with lemon wedges and green salad to 6.

FRITTO MISTO #2
Mixed Fry #2

1 pound whitebait
1 pound squid, cleaned at fish market
Flour
Corn or peanut oil

Leave fish intact if small. If fish is over 2 inches long, remove stomach. Wash fish and blot with paper towels. Cut squid into ½-inch pieces. Dust fish in flour. Cook in hot corn or peanut oil as in Fritto Misto #1. Serves 4.

ABOUT BRODETTO

One summer a couple of years ago, we invited some new friends to our summer place in Provincetown, on Cape Cod, for a fish dinner. They enjoyed the dinner and apparently described it to their friend Hans Hoffman, the marvelous teacher and painter. Mr. Hoffman, who also lived in Provincetown during the summer, was in his seventies and loved fish, especially shellfish. Hearing about the dinner I had cooked, he said: "Tell your young artist friend I can come over next Tuesday at seven P.M.!" I was, it goes without saying, delighted to have Mr. Hoffman as a guest, and I cooked the best shellfish and seafood dinner I could manage. We had been told that since the death of his wife Mr. Hoffman hated to be in a closed room, so we served dinner on our terrace under an old grape arbor. He seemed to enjoy it thoroughly. He was in wonderful form and talked for hours about his experiences in the Bauhaus and in Paris.

We invited Mr. Hoffman a number of times after that night. I remember especially one lovely May afternoon when he came to our house in Katonah. I cooked a *brodetto* of fresh asparagus and fish. Again, we ate outdoors under a very old wisteria arbor, with the fragrant blossoms hanging like huge bunches of grapes above us. The last time we had dinner together was in Provincetown a few months before he died. I cooked Wellfleet oysters and chicken with squid and mussels and we ate again under that Cape Cod grape arbor. Mr. Hoffman fascinated us for hours with his stories of Paris and of Picasso, whom he knew as a young man. I remember thinking how really young Hoffman was, as his paintings clearly show. He was ageless and was a lesson to us all on how beautiful old age can be.

BRODETTO ALLA MARCHIGIANA #1
Fish Stew, Marchigiana Style #1

2 pounds mussels
18 small clams
1 pound raw shrimp
1 pound squid, cleaned at the fish market
1 large bunch fresh broccoli or asparagus
6 slices (not fillets) striped bass*
Butter

SAUCE

½ cup olive oil
1 red or green pepper, chopped
¼ cup minced parsley, Italian if possible
2 cloves garlic, minced
3 small ripe tomatoes, coarsely chopped
2 teaspoons chopped mint
4 tablespoons chopped fresh basil or 1 tablespoon dried basil
Pinch hot pepper (optional)
½ cup dry white wine

Scrub mussels well under running water with a hard brush, preferably wire. Scrape off any encrustations on the shells and cut off the beards. Scrub the clams too. Remove shells and de-vein shrimp. Wash the squid and cut in ½-inch strips. Clean and trim the broccoli and drop into boiling salted water for 3 minutes. Drain. Set all aside while you prepare the sauce.

Preheat oven to 400°. Pour the oil into a large flat roasting tray to coat the bottom lightly. Scatter all vegetables and herbs

* You can use cod or haddock.

over the oil, then add the wine. Place in oven and bake until peppers are tender—a matter of minutes.

Now add the other stew ingredients in the following order: First, the mussels and clams; when they open, remove and set aside. Add the bass; dot the fish generously with butter. After 5 minutes, add the squid. After 5 more minutes, add the shrimp and finally the clams and mussels. Cook another 10 minutes.

Serve immediately from the pan in which the brodetto was cooked to 8 to 10.

BRODETTO ALLA MARCHIGIANA #2
Fish Stew, Marchigiana Style #2

1 pound mussels
1 pound striped bass,* sliced
¾ pound whiting** cut in half
1 fillet of flounder cut into 1-inch slices
½ pound raw shrimp
1 pound squid
1 large onion, chopped
4 tablespoons olive oil
Salt and freshly ground black pepper
½ cup chopped parsley
1 tablespoon fresh sage or 1 teaspoon dried sage
½ cup dry white wine
½ cup water
½ teaspoon saffron diluted in 1 tablespoon warm water
1 French or Italian bread
2 cloves garlic

Scrub the mussels thoroughly under running water. Wash the fish. Shell and de-vein shrimp. Wash squid and cut into ½-inch pieces. Sauté onion in oil in a wide skillet. When the onion

---

* Slice of striped bass should be about 1 inch thick.

** If these fish are not available, substitute white-meat fish which are in season.

begins to wilt, add squid and salt and pepper to taste. Turn up heat and cook for 5 minutes. Lower heat and add parsley and sage. Cook 10 minutes longer, then add wine and water. Cover and simmer for 5 minutes. Add mussels, cover and cook until they open. Add bass and cook, covered, over moderate heat for 5 minutes. Add whiting, partially cover skillet and cook for 5 minutes longer. Add flounder, shrimp and saffron. Cover and cook until shrimp are tender.

Cover the bottom of another large skillet with olive oil. Use about 2 slices of French or Italian bread per person and rub bread with split clove of garlic. Put into skillet and fry on both sides until brown. Place fried bread slices on each plate and spoon fish and sauce on top. Serves 4 to 6.

BRODETTO ALLA SAN BENEDETTO
Fish Stew San Benedetto Style

½ pound squid, cleaned at fish market
2 medium whiting,* with heads on
1 pound striped bass*
12 mussels
½ pound raw shrimp
6 clams
1 medium onion, plus 2 tablespoons, chopped
½ cup, plus 2 tablespoons, olive oil
4 tablespoons chopped parsley, Italian if possible
½ green pepper, pickled in vinegar if possible
¼ cup wine vinegar
¾ cup chopped tomato
Salt and hot pepper
¼ cup dry white wine

Wash squid and all fish. Cut whiting and bass into 3-inch pieces, squid into ½-inch pieces. Scrub the mussels well under

---

* If these fish are not available, substitute other white-meat fish which are in season.

running water. Shell and de-vein shrimp. Sauté squid and all but 2 tablespoons of the onion in 2 tablespoons of the olive oil in a small skillet for 5 minutes. When onion looks wilted, set the mixture aside. Do not overcook.

Meanwhile, place remaining olive oil and onion, 3 tablespoons of the parsley, and green pepper in a large skillet. Cook over high flame for several minutes, and add vinegar. Cook for several minutes and add tomato, salt and hot pepper to taste and continue cooking, uncovered, for 5 minutes. Add bass and cook for 5 more minutes. Add whiting and cook for several minutes. Add clams and cook for several minutes. Add mussels and cook until they begin to open, then add the shrimp. As soon as shrimp change color, add wine. Cover and simmer for about 5 minutes, add remaining parsley and simmer a few minutes more. Serve hot over toasted French or Italian bread to 6.

STOCCAFISSO
Sun-Dried Stockfish (Cod)

This is an unsalted dried codfish. It is brought to this country from Scandinavia or Iceland and is very popular in Mediterranean countries. It is available in Italian markets. Make sure it's fresh.

Place fish in pot large enough to hold it, but if necessary, saw fish in half. Soak in cold running water if possible. If not, change water very often, at least 4 times a day. Soak the fish for 4 days and nights. At this point fish is ready for cooking. Drain it well.

STOCCAFISSO CON SEDANO E PATATE
Dried Stockfish with Celery and Potatoes

1½ pounds stockfish
6 tablespoons olive oil
1 cup chopped onion
2 cloves garlic, chopped
½ cup dry white wine
3 stalks celery, cut into 2-inch pieces
2 cups peeled and chopped tomatoes
5 small potatoes, cut in half, lengthwise
3 tablespoons chopped parsley, Italian if possible
1 tablespoon chopped sweet basil
Salt and hot or freshly ground black pepper

Preheat oven to 450°.
Pre-soak fish according to above instructions and cut into 3-inch pieces. Place 4 tablespoons of the olive oil in a broad ovenproof pan. Lay fish on bottom of pan, sprinkle with chopped onion and garlic. Place pan in oven without cover, and bake until onions begin to brown. Do not stir. Add wine and bake until wine is absorbed. Arrange celery around fish and add tomatoes and potatoes. Sprinkle with parsley, basil, salt and pepper to taste. Cover tightly and bake for 10 minutes. Lower heat to 400° and bake for ½ hour. Add the remaining 2 tablespoons of olive oil and bake for 20 minutes. Serve hot to 6.

BACCALÀ
Dried Salted Cod

To pre-soak baccalà use same procedure as for stocca-fisso (page 102), but soak baccalà for 2 days only. Of course, since baccalà is salted, you must be careful with the amount of salt you use in cooking.

CROCCHETTE DI BACCALÀ
Dried Salted Cod Croquettes

1 pound dried salted cod (baccalà)
1 clove garlic
2 cups mashed potatoes, freshly cooked
1 tablespoon finely chopped parsley, Italian if possible
3 eggs
Freshly ground black pepper
3 tablespoons grated Parmesan cheese
1 cup fresh bread crumbs
Corn oil
Lemon wedges

Pre-soak codfish according to instructions on page 103. Drain the cod and place it in a saucepan. Add enough cold water to cover. Add garlic and bring to a boil. Simmer 15 minutes. Drain fish, discard garlic and cool.

Shred the cod, discarding any bits of skin and bones. Blend cod with mashed potatoes, parsley, 2 of the eggs, lightly beaten, pepper to taste and cheese. Shape the cod mixture into tube-shaped croquettes, about 3 inches long and 1 inch in diameter. Roll the croquettes in beaten egg, then coat them with crumbs.

Pour about 1 inch of corn oil into a skillet. When oil is hot, fry the croquettes until golden brown on all sides. Drain on paper towels and serve hot with lemon wedges to 4.

BACCALÀ CON BROCCOLI DI RAPE
Dried Salted Cod with Rape

2 pounds dried salted cod (baccalà)
⅔ cup olive oil, plus 2 tablespoons
2 pounds of rape
2 cloves garlic, sliced
Salt and freshly ground black pepper or hot pepper
½ cup dried black olives

Pre-soak cod according to instructions on page 103 and cut into 2-inch squares. Preheat oven to 450°. Pour ⅔ cup of the olive oil into shallow baking pan. Add cod and place in oven. Bake 15 minutes.

While fish bakes, drop rape into a saucepan of boiling water. When water returns to a boil, remove rape and drain. In a pot combine remaining 2 tablespoons olive oil, garlic, salt and pepper to taste. Cook over high heat for 10 minutes.

Add olives to cod and return to oven. Bake for 20 minutes, turning occasionally. Lower heat to 375°. Add rape to baccalà and put back in oven. Bake, uncovered, for 20 minutes. Leave in oven for 5 minutes after heat is turned off. Taste for seasoning and add salt if necessary. Serves 6 to 8.

LUMACHE ALLA MARCHIGIANA
Snails Marchigiana

This dish is quite a lot of trouble to make, but if you have the time, it is delicious and worth the trouble.

1 pound live snails in the shell
1 cup wine vinegar
3 tablespoons salt
¼ cup olive oil
½ cup chopped green pepper
2 cloves garlic, crushed
1 teaspoon sage
1 teaspoon rosemary
2 bay leaves
1 tablespoon chopped parsley, Italian if possible
½ teaspoon dried mint
Freshly ground black pepper
½ teaspoon oregano
1 teaspoon chopped sweet basil
¼ cup dry white wine
¾ cup seeded tomato

Place snails in a kettle with enough cold water to cover. Cover the kettle securely.

When the snails push out from their shell (they will still be attached, of course) use the back of a heavy knife to knock a small hole in the side of each shell. Wash each shell and set them aside in a colander to drain. Discard any shells from which snails did not peek out.* Combine the vinegar and salt and wash the snails in the mixture, stirring them constantly until the mixture thickens, about 10 minutes. Discard the slime and rinse the snails in cold water. Continue rinsing snails until water is clear.

Place snails in a kettle and cover with cold water. Set aside.

---

* The snails are still in shells. In this recipe, snails are cooked in shells and served in shells.

When some of the snails begin to come out of their shells again, place the pot over low flame. (All the snails will not come out this time.) When water in kettle starts to boil, drain the snails without letting them cook.

Place the oil in a skillet large enough to hold the snails. Heat briefly and add the snails. Simmer, stirring, about 1 minute. Add all the remaining ingredients, except the wine and tomatoes. Simmer 10 minutes and add the wine. Cover and cook over medium high heat for about 5 minutes. Remove the cover, lower the heat and let simmer 5 minutes.

In a separate saucepan cook the tomatoes about 4 minutes. Add them to the snails and cover. Simmer 20 to 25 minutes, adding a little hot water if the sauce becomes too thick. Serve hot as a first course with toothpicks or other food picks to get the snails out of shells. The sauce is excellent to dip pieces of Italian bread in. Serves 4.

POLLAME
e selvaggina
Poultry and Game

Lisa Gibbi

About

POULTRY

My mother and father never bought a "dead chicken." They always bought live chickens at a Jewish poultry market. They would bring the bird home, feathers and all, and pluck it in our yard, but after my mother got to know the man who ran the market she trusted him to do the plucking—and to deliver her the same chicken she'd picked.

I keep my own chickens now, laying-hens which I use for soup chickens after they stop producing. The children don't like the idea, and Lisa, who is seven, is especially sensitive about hurting animals and birds. She loves them all and says she is going to grow up to be a "Sagittarius," but I think she means a vegetarian.

CAPPONE FARCITO
Stuffed Capon

1 medium-sized surgical capon*
2 cloves garlic
Olive oil
1 tablespoon fresh rosemary
Salt and freshly ground black pepper
1 cup dry white wine
4 strips salt pork

STUFFING

Capon gizzard, diced
2 small onions, chopped
1 tablespoon butter
1 cup grated Parmesan or pecorino cheese
½ cup chopped parsley
1 capon liver (raw), diced
2 tablespoons raisins
2 tablespoons chopped walnuts
2 cups bread crumbs
1 tablespoon chopped fresh basil or 1 teaspoon dried basil
1 teaspoon thyme
2 eggs, lightly beaten

Preheat oven to 400°.

To make stuffing, sauté gizzard and onions in butter until onions wilt, adding more butter, if necessary. Cut gizzard in cubes—discard tough parts. Mix together all remaining stuffing ingredients. Stuff bird. Cut garlic in slivers and slip under skin of capon (remember to discard when chicken is roasted).

Truss the bird, then rub with a little olive oil, rosemary, salt

---

* A surgical capon is a rooster that has been castrated surgically. Other capons are the result of hormone injections. I personally frown upon the use of hormones in food, and though surgical capons are more expensive, they are worth it.

and pepper to taste. Place strips of salt pork over bird. Roast capon on rack in shallow baking pan. When capon is brown, add wine by pouring over bird and allowing to collect in pan. Cover pan and lower heat to 350°. Baste often, and roast for about 1½ hours, or until tender. Serves 6 to 8.

Meat Stuffing for Roast Capon or Chicken

½ pound ground pork
½ pound ground lean chuck
2 tablespoons butter
1 small onion, chopped
Salt and freshly ground black pepper
½ cup dry white wine
1 teaspoon dried basil
2 tablespoons minced parsley, Italian if possible
½ cup bread crumbs
¼ cup milk
Chicken liver, diced
1 egg, lightly beaten
½ cup grated Parmesan or Romano cheese
Dash of nutmeg

Sauté both ground meats in butter in an uncovered skillet over medium heat, stirring often. As meats turn color, add onions. When meats begin to brown, add salt and pepper to taste, wine, basil and parsley. Cover, lower heat, and simmer until wine evaporates.

Meanwhile, soak bread crumbs in milk. Wash and coarsely chop chicken liver. In a large bowl, combine cooked meats and their pan juices with bread crumbs, uncooked chicken liver and remaining ingredients. Add salt and pepper to correct seasoning. Mix well. Stuffing is now ready for the bird.

POLLO IN CRETA
Chicken Baked in Clay

I learned to prepare chicken in clay from a friend in Florence. The original recipe called for a freshly killed chicken, with its feathers on and its cavity cleaned. The clay was applied over the feathers and then baked. When the hard clay was removed, the feathers came off with it. Once, when I made this recipe, I overcooked the chicken, and the skin also came off with the feathers, but even so, the meat was excellent. The feathers do have a disagreeable odor when the clay is opened but the taste is not affected. However, the following recipe is easier for the modern cook to manage.

A 3- to 4-pound chicken
1 clove garlic
1 teaspoon rosemary
Salt and freshly ground black pepper
1 tablespoon olive oil or butter
1 teaspoon thyme
1 tablespoon pesto, optional (page 217)
Sculptors' clay to cover chicken 1 inch thick*

SAUCE

½ medium onion, finely chopped
2 tablespoons butter
1 cup Marsala wine

Wash and soak chicken in salted cold water to cover for 1 hour. Rinse, drain and pat dry with paper towels. Preheat oven to 350°. Cut garlic in slivers and slip under skin of chicken. (Remember to discard when chicken is baked.) Place rosemary and salt and pepper to taste in chicken cavity. Rub oil or butter over the bird and sprinkle with thyme, salt and pepper. Spread pesto over the breasts.

Wrap chicken neatly in foil, then cover with a 1-inch-thick

* Be certain to use earth clay, not Plasticine.

coating of clay. Be careful to spread the clay firmly and evenly. (If you like, you can sculpt the clay into the form of a chicken, or have some children make a bird form after the clay is applied.)

Place the chicken in a shallow baking pan and put in the oven to bake. After 45 minutes, increase the heat to 400°, and bake 15 minutes. Look into the oven from time to time, and if the clay cracks and steam escapes, stuff the crack with more clay. Remove the chicken from the oven after 1 hour. You can paint the clay with water color or poster paint for a very handsome presentation.

To make the sauce, sauté onion in butter. When onion wilts, add wine and cook, uncovered, over medium heat until liquid is reduced by half. While the sauce is cooking, show your guests the clay-covered bird. Then crack the clay open, remove chicken and take it out of the foil. Save the liquid in the foil and add it to the wine-and-onion mixture. Simmer over low heat while you carve the chicken into serving pieces. Pour the sauce over the chicken and serve immediately to 4 to 6.

POLLO AI FERRI
Broiled Chicken

A 2- to 3-pound fryer, split
Juice of 3 lemons or 4 tablespoons wine vinegar
2 cloves garlic, sliced
4 tablespoons olive oil
2 tablespoons chopped parsley
1 tablespoon crushed rosemary leaves
Salt and freshly ground black pepper

Soak chicken for 1 hour in cold salted water. Rinse, then marinate in a mixture of the remaining ingredients for at least one hour. Broil chicken on both sides over hot coals or under broiler unit, basting often with the marinade. Broil for about 45 minutes, or until tender. Serves 3 or 4.

POLLO IN SALE
Chicken Cooked in Salt

My mother sent me this recipe from Italy. It is a bland but surprisingly tasty dish that is served to people who are ill.

A 3-pound chicken
1 tablespoon rosemary
2 cloves garlic, finely sliced
3 pounds coarse kosher salt

Preheat oven to 400°. Rub inside of chicken with rosemary. Place garlic slices under skin of chicken breasts (remember to discard when chicken is cooked).

Fill inside of cavity with half the salt. Cover with a layer of salt the bottom of a baking pan large enough to hold chicken. Place the chicken in bed of salt, pour remaining salt over chicken and pat it down. Cover and place in oven. Bake 15 minutes and lower heat to 375°. Bake 1 hour or until chicken is tender. Do not overcook, because salt will dry out the meat. Remove chicken from pan. Brush salt off and remove the skin. Carve chicken and serve hot to 4.

POLLO CON ASPARAGI E MARSALA
Chicken with Asparagus and Marsala

A 3-pound fryer, cut in pieces
2 ounces packaged dried Italian mushrooms
1½ pounds fresh asparagus
2 tablespoons olive oil
2 tablespoons butter
½ tablespoon crushed rosemary
2 onions, chopped
½ cup dry Marsala, imported if possible
½ tablespoon thyme
Salt and freshly ground black pepper

Soak chicken in cold salted water for 1 hour. Rinse, drain and dry with paper towels. Soak mushrooms according to instructions on package. Wash asparagus. Break off tough ends and cut into 2-inch pieces. Drain and set aside.

Preheat oven to 400°. Sauté chicken in heated olive oil and butter in a large skillet. Sauté, uncovered, over moderate heat, turning occasionally. After 15 minutes add rosemary. When chicken begins to brown, add onion, asparagus, drained mushrooms, salt and pepper to taste. Cook until onion wilts. Then add wine* and thyme. Place in oven and bake for about 15 minutes. Serves 4 to 6.

* If chicken is fat, drain off most of fat before adding wine.

POLLO CON CAVOLFIORE
Chicken with Cauliflower

A 3-pound fryer, cut in pieces
3 tablespoons olive oil
3 cloves garlic, unpeeled
Salt and freshly ground black pepper
1 head of cauliflower, broken into flowerets*
¼ cup wine vinegar
1 tablespoon chopped rosemary
1 tablespoon chopped parsley, Italian if possible
½ cup chopped tomato
½ can (pitted) black olives, drained

Sauté chicken in olive oil with garlic and salt and pepper to taste over moderate heat in wide uncovered skillet. Turn pieces occasionally. While chicken is cooking, blanch cauliflower in boiling water. Drain and set aside, but keep warm. When chicken is brown, add vinegar, rosemary and parsley. Cover, lower heat and simmer for 3 minutes. Take off cover, turn up heat and boil until the vinegar has evaporated. Add tomatoes, and when they begin to boil, add black olives and cauliflower. Cover, and simmer 15 to 20 minutes. Discard garlic. Serves 6.

* Or you can use 1 pound of Brussels sprouts.

POLLO CON CASTAGNE
Chicken with Chestnuts

A 3-pound fryer, cut in pieces
3 tablespoons olive oil
Salt and freshly ground black pepper
1 onion, chopped
1 clove garlic, chopped
1 cup sliced fresh mushrooms
¾ cup dry Marsala, imported if possible
1 tablespoon rosemary
1 teaspoon thyme
12 fresh chestnuts
2 tablespoons butter

Sauté chicken in olive oil, turning the pieces often. Add salt and pepper to taste. When chicken is brown, add onions, garlic and mushrooms. Cook until onion wilts, then add Marsala, rosemary and thyme. Cover, lower heat and simmer for 5 minutes.

While chicken is cooking, split each chestnut and boil in water to cover for 5 minutes. Remove shells, cut chestnuts in half and add to chicken. Stir in butter and simmer gently for 15 minutes. Serves 4 to 6.

POLLO CON PATATE E ROSMARINO
Chicken with Potatoes and Rosemary

A 3-pound chicken, cut in pieces
4 tablespoons olive oil
2 cloves garlic, chopped
1 cup dry white wine
2 tablespoons chopped rosemary
2 bay leaves
4 cups potatoes, cut into ¼-inch slices
Salt and freshly ground black pepper

Preheat oven to 400°.
Wash and dry chicken. Sauté chicken pieces and garlic in 2

tablespoons of the olive oil, over medium heat, in uncovered ovenproof casserole. Turn chicken often. When chicken begins to brown, drain off most of the oil. Add wine, rosemary and bay leaves. Cover and simmer for 5 minutes. Add potatoes and salt and pepper to taste. Cover and place in oven. Bake, stirring occasionally, until potatoes are tender, about 25 minutes. Add a little chicken stock or warm water if necessary, though this dish should be rather dry. (Potatoes will disintegrate to a certain extent.) Serves 4 to 6.

POLLO CANZANESE
Chicken Canzanese

This dish is from the Abruzzi region, and the recipe was given to my mother by a woman from Canzano.

A 3-pound chicken, cut in pieces
2 sage leaves
2 bay leaves
1 clove garlic, sliced lengthwise
6 whole cloves
2 springs fresh rosemary or ½ teaspoon dried rosemary
12 peppercorns, crushed
1 hot red pepper, broken and seeded (optional)
¼ pound prosciutto, sliced ½ inch thick
½ cup dry white wine
¼ cup water

Cut chicken into serving pieces and soak in salted cold water to cover for 1 hour. Rinse, drain and dry with paper towels.

Arrange the chicken pieces in one layer in a skillet. Add the sage, bay leaves, garlic, whole cloves, rosemary, peppercorns and red pepper. Cut the prosciutto into small cubes and sprinkle it over the chicken. Add the wine and water. Do not salt, since the prosciutto will season the dish. Cover and simmer 40 minutes. Uncover and cook briefly over high heat until sauce is reduced slightly. Serves 4.

POLLO CON PISELLI
Chicken with Peas

A 3-pound chicken
2 tablespoons olive oil
Salt and freshly ground black pepper
1 tablespoon rosemary
1 cup finely chopped onion
½ cup dry white wine
1 teaspoon dried thyme
2 cups green or canned peas*
1 cup chopped tomato, drained
¼ cup butter
2 tablespoons finely chopped parsley, Italian if possible
Grated Parmesan cheese

Cut chicken into serving pieces and soak in salted cold water to cover for 1 hour. Rinse, drain and dry with paper towels.

Preheat oven to 400°. Heat the oil in a wide skillet and cook the chicken over moderate heat, about 5 minutes, turning often. Sprinkle with salt and pepper to taste and rosemary. Continue cooking, uncovered, until chicken starts to brown. Add the onion, and when it wilts, pour off and discard most of the oil from the skillet. Add the wine and thyme, cover and simmer about 5 minutes. Uncover and cook over high heat until most of the wine has evaporated.

Meanwhile, place fresh peas in a saucepan and add water to cover. Add salt to taste, and simmer until tender. Set aside. Add the tomato, butter and drained peas to the chicken. Sprinkle with parsley, cover and bake 15 minutes. Serve sprinkled with Parmesan cheese, with rice as an accompaniment, to 6.

* Cooked cannellini beans or fava or lima beans may be substituted for the peas and added to the chicken with the tomatoes and butter.

POLLO CON COZZE
Chicken with Mussels

½ cup olive oil
A 2- to 3-pound chicken, cut in serving pieces
4 whole cloves garlic
1½ cups dry white wine
1 teaspoon dried oregano
1 tablespoon chopped sweet basil
1 teaspoon rosemary
1 teaspoon chopped mint
2 cups peeled, seeded and coarsely chopped tomatoes
1 green pepper, chopped
¼ cup minced parsley, Italian if possible
2 pounds mussels*
Salt and hot red pepper

Heat oil in large skillet, add chicken and cook over moderate heat, turning often. After 5 minutes, add garlic. When chicken is brown, add wine and herbs. Cover, lower heat, and cook for 5 minutes. Uncover, turn up heat and cook until the wine evaporates. Add tomatoes, green pepper, parsley, salt and pepper to taste. Cover, raise the heat, and when liquid boils, remove the cover and cook over moderate heat until sauce thickens. Stir with wooden spoon occasionally. Scrub mussels thoroughly under cold running water and add them to chicken. Cook until mussel shells open. Remove chicken and mussels and discard garlic cloves. If sauce is too watery reduce over high heat. Pour over chicken and serve immediately to 8.

* Shrimp may be used instead of, or with, mussels.

POLLO CON SCAMPI E PISELLI
Chicken with Shrimp and Peas

This recipe is an excellent way to use leftover soup chicken.

1 pound raw shrimp
1 cup coarsely chopped boiled chicken
1 cup coarsely chopped tomato
1 teaspoon oregano
1 cup canned or cooked fresh peas
Salt and freshly ground black pepper
3 tablespoons butter
¾ cup chopped onion
1 teaspoon minced garlic
Juice of ½ lemon
½ teaspoon chopped mint
Hot pepper

Shell and de-vein shrimp. Place chicken in a wide skillet with tomato, oregano, peas and salt and pepper to taste. Cook, uncovered, over high heat for 5 minutes.

Meanwhile, in a separate skillet, sauté onion in butter over high heat for several minutes. Add shrimp and continue to cook, uncovered, over high heat for 3 to 4 minutes, or until shrimp are cooked. Then add lemon juice. Cook several minutes, and add to chicken and peas. Stir in hot pepper to taste. Cover and cook over low heat for 5 minutes. Serve hot on rice to 4.

ALE DI POLLO CON POMODORI E CIPOLLE
Chicken Wings with Tomatoes and Onions

8 chicken wings, separated at joints
3 tablespoons olive oil
Salt and freshly ground black pepper
1 clove garlic, chopped
½ cup chopped onion
½ cup dry white wine
1 teaspoon rosemary
½ cup chopped tomato

Sauté chicken in oil over moderate heat, uncovered, and turn often. Add salt and pepper to taste. When chicken wings begin to brown, add garlic and onion. Cook until onion is limp, then add wine and rosemary. Cover, and simmer for 5 minutes. Add tomato, re-cover, and cook, over moderate heat, for 15 minutes more. Serve with rice to 2.

PICCIONE ALLA CACCIATORA
Squab Hunter Style

3 squab
3 tablespoons pancetta*
1 tablespoon butter
2 bay leaves
½ teaspoon sage
Salt and freshly ground black pepper
1 teaspoon minced garlic
3 tablespoons chopped prosciutto
½ cup dry white wine
2 cups sliced fresh mushrooms**
1 cup chicken stock
1 tablespoon tomato paste
Risotto (page 64)

Preheat oven to 450°. Split each squab in half. Wash and pat dry with paper towels.

Heat pancetta and butter together in a large skillet. Add squab, bay leaves, sage and salt and pepper to taste. Cook, uncovered, over medium heat, turning often. After 15 minutes, add garlic and prosciutto. Cook several minutes, stirring with a wooden spoon. Then add wine and mushrooms. Cover, lower heat, and cook 5 to 7 minutes. Add stock and tomato paste. Cover skillet with foil and place in oven. Bake for 45 minutes. Serve hot with risotto to 3.

* Sweet pickled pork or bacon can be used as a substitute.

** If fresh mushrooms are not available, you can use 1 cup dried Italian mushrooms soaked in warm water for 15 minutes and drained.

ANITRELLA CON OLIVE
Duckling with Olives

A 5-pound duckling
Salt and freshly ground black pepper to taste
1 tablespoon rosemary
1 medium apple
1 tablespoon olive oil
2 medium onions
1 cup dry white wine
1 cup beef or chicken stock
Butter
¾ pound dried, water-cured Greek or Italian black olives

Preheat oven to 425°.

In the cavity of the duckling put salt, pepper, rosemary and the whole, unpeeled apple. Truss and rub the duckling with olive oil, salt and pepper, and place it in an ovenproof pot that holds it comfortably. Arrange onions alongside the duckling. Place pot, uncovered, in oven and bake until duckling is a golden-brown, basting often. Most of the fat beneath the skin should be cooked out and the skin should be crisp. Place the cover of the pot on a piece of brown paper and trace its outline, then cut out the paper shape and set it aside. Pour off fat from pot and add wine and duckling giblets to pot. Return to oven, cover and cook about 10 minutes, basting often. After most of the wine evaporates, add stock. Butter the paper cutout and place it over the duckling. Cover pot again and continue to bake for 30 minutes, basting occasionally. In the meantime, peel meat off olive pits in a spiral fashion, as you would an orange rind. Add olives to duckling and cook, covered, 10 minutes more.

Remove duckling from pot, cut in serving pieces and place on a heated platter. Pour sauce over duckling and serve immediately to 5 to 6.

ANITRELLA CON LENTICCHIE
Duckling with Lentils

A 4-pound duckling
Salt and freshly ground black pepper to taste
½ cup cubed salt pork
2 tablespoons olive oil
1 medium onion, chopped
2 cloves garlic, chopped
½ cup chopped celery
½ cup chopped carrot
3 tablespoons fresh minced parsley, Italian if possible
2 bay leaves
¾ cup dry white wine

Wash and dry the whole duckling and sprinkle it with salt and pepper. Sauté duckling in a large skillet with the salt pork and olive oil over moderate heat. When duckling begins to brown, add onion and garlic and simmer until onion wilts. Add celery, carrots, parsley and bay leaves. Cover and simmer until vegetables are tender. Add wine and simmer until wine evaporates. Add enough hot water to cover duckling. Cook over high heat, until water boils. Lower heat so that water boils gently, and cook 1 hour or until duckling is tender. Skim fat from liquid and save for stock. Now prepare the lentils.

LENTILS

2 tablespoons olive oil
2 small onions, chopped
Duckling's liver, chopped
4 cups stock from duckling
⅓ cup chopped carrot
1 teaspoon sweet basil
½ cup chopped celery
1 cup lentils
Salt and freshly ground black pepper to taste

Sauté onion in olive oil. When onion wilts, add chopped liver. When liver loses its color, add stock, carrot, basil, and celery. When liquid comes to a boil, add lentils, salt and pepper. Cover and simmer, adding more liquid if necessary.

When lentils are tender, in about 20 minutes, remove duckling from sauce and cut up. Place on heated serving platter with lentils. Serve hot to 6.

ABOUT GAME

That my father loved to cook game was known in the area where we lived and hunters would bring their catch to him. Sometimes they would just leave it with him, sometimes they would join us for dinner. My father would look at the meat and decide how long it should be marinated and how it should be cooked. His recipes were simple, usually with wild mushrooms, wine, garlic and oil.

I often think about a day in 1955 when my father decided it was time to come to New York to visit me. At the time, I was painting—but not selling—living in Hell's Kitchen in a cold-water flat and living very frugally. That morning my mother called me and told me to expect Pop at about eleven o'clock on the train from Waterbury.

When he arrived, he had a large cardboard box under each arm. One box contained a fresh-killed chicken (he never bought "dead" chickens), a gallon of his own wine and a large loaf of Italian bread. The other box contained a jar of home-canned wild mushrooms, a quart of my mother's spaghetti sauce, a pound of imported Italian pasta, pecorino cheese his brother had made in Italy, some salami, homemade biscotti, and home-canned tomatoes.

After displaying this bounty, my father cooked the chicken with tomatoes and wild mushrooms and, with the wine and bread, we had a feast. After lunch we went to a gallery on Madison Avenue and 77th Street where there was an exhibit of my drawings. When we left the exhibition I tried to think of something to do that would please Pop. Knowing his love for animals, I thought he would enjoy the zoo at Central Park. We first went to see the big animals—the lions and tigers, etc. My father seemed bored and I began to worry that the excursion had not been a good idea after all. But at that moment, we got to the area where the small North American animals are kept. To my surprise, my father's face lit up. When we came to the cage with the raccoons, he said, "You know, you would have to marinate them in wine for about four hours before you cook them." Then we walked up to the cage of an opossum and he said, "That one looks tough. I think I would marinate him in vinegar and water overnight." At the next cage he said, "I'd cook that one in a nice tight sauce with wild mushrooms."

He was perfectly serious. He had finally found animals he could relate to. Most of my father's life was spent in hard work so that there would be enough food on his family's table, and to me, knowing this, and thinking of my own poverty at the time, his reaction to the animals made sense. Pop would even describe people in relation to food. One day when I was a child he was talking about a man with a large nose. He said, "He must have had a nose that weighed two pounds." It seemed the largest nose in the world to me. Imagine, a man with a two-pound nose!

FAGIANO CON MARSALA E BRANDY
Pheasant with Marsala and Brandy

1 large pheasant
Flour
2 tablespoons olive oil
2 tablespoons butter
2 whole cloves garlic
2 bay leaves
Salt and freshly ground black pepper
¾ cup imported dry Marsala
1 cup dried Italian mushrooms
1 teaspoon thyme
¼ cup brandy

Cut up pheasant as you would a frying chicken. Soak bird in salted cold water for 1 hour. Rinse and dry with paper towels. Dust with flour. Soak mushrooms in warm water for 15 minutes. Heat oil and butter in a wide skillet, add pheasant and increase the heat. Turn each piece after several minutes, add garlic, bay leaves, salt and pepper to taste. Cook, uncovered, over high heat, stirring constantly, until liquid from bird evaporates.

Lower heat. Add ½ cup of the wine, drained mushrooms and thyme. Cover and simmer for 5 minutes, then raise heat to medium. Cook, stirring occasionally until pheasant is almost tender. Add the rest of the wine and cook for about 10 minutes more. Add brandy and cook over high heat for several minutes. Remove to serving platter, discard garlic and serve hot to 6.
Note: Do not cook too long or the meat will dry out.

FAGIANO AL MODO MIO
Pheasant My Way

1 fat pheasant
½ cup (¾-ounce) dried Italian mushrooms or 1 cup fresh
    mushrooms
3 tablespoons olive oil
3 whole cloves garlic
2 bay leaves
Salt and freshly ground black pepper
½ cup finely chopped onion
¼ cup chopped prosciutto
⅔ cup dry white wine
1 teaspoon rosemary
½ teaspoon dried mint or 1 tablespoon chopped fresh mint
⅔ cup tomatoes, strained

Soak pheasant in salted cold water for 2 hours. Cut in serving
pieces as you would a frying chicken. If dried mushrooms are
used, soak them in warm water for 15 minutes. Heat olive oil in
a wide skillet and add pheasant. Cook, uncovered, over medium
heat, stirring often. Add garlic, bay leaves and salt and pepper to
taste. When pheasant begins to brown, stir in onion, prosciutto
and mushrooms. Continue to stir often with a wooden spoon.
When onion wilts, add wine, rosemary and mint. Cover, lower
heat and simmer about 7 minutes. Add tomatoes and continue to
cook, covered, for about 30 minutes or until tender. Discard
garlic. Serves 4 to 6.

MALLARDO AL MARSALA
Mallard with Marsala

1 mallard
4 tablespoons olive oil or butter
Salt and freshly ground black pepper
2 medium onions, chopped
1 carrot, chopped
½ cup dry imported Marsala
2 whole cloves garlic
1 bay leaf
1 teaspoon oregano
1 teaspoon rosemary
1 teaspoon tomato paste
½ cup warm stock or water

Soak mallard in salted cold water for 2 hours.
Preheat oven to 400°.
Sauté whole duck in oil or butter in an ovenproof casserole over medium heat. Add salt and pepper to taste. When duck is brown on all sides, add onion and carrot. When onion wilts, add wine, garlic, bay leaf, oregano and rosemary. Cover, lower heat, and cook for 5 minutes. Then add tomato paste and warm stock and bring to a boil.

Place casserole in oven and bake, covered, for about 1½ hours,* or until tender. Baste often, adding more stock if necessary. To serve, cut bird into serving pieces, arrange on platter and pour sauce over it, first discarding garlic. Serve hot to 4.

* Cooking time depends on size of duck.

TETRAONE CON PESTO
Grouse with Pesto

1 fat grouse
1 whole clove garlic
1 teaspoon rosemary
1 bay leaf
Salt and freshly ground black pepper
2 slices prosciutto or salt pork, about 2 inches wide and 3
    inches long
⅔ cup dry white wine

Preheat oven to 400°.

Stuff bird with garlic, rosemary, bay leaf, salt and pepper to taste. Tie prosciutto or salt pork on outside of bird and bake for 30 minutes or until bird begins to brown, basting often. Add wine, cover and cook another 5 to 10 minutes. In the meantime make sauce:

SAUCE

½ cup dried Italian mushrooms or ½ cup sliced fresh mush-
    rooms
⅓ cup chopped onion
2 tablespoons butter
Giblets of grouse, cut into ¼-inch slices
⅔ cup dry white wine
½ teaspoon dried mint or 1 tablespoon chopped fresh mint
1 tablespoon pesto (see Pesto #2, page 218), diluted in 1 ta-
    blespoon warm water
Salt and freshly ground black pepper

If dried mushrooms are used, soak in warm water for 15 minutes. Sauté onion in butter. After 1 minute, add giblets and mushrooms. When onion wilts, add wine, mint, pesto, salt and pepper to taste. Cover and cook over low heat, stirring often, for 5 to 10 minutes. Set aside and keep warm.

Take cover off the grouse and cook out most of wine. Then add sauce, cover and return to oven 10 minutes. Serve hot to 2.

CONIGLIO IN GIALMI
Rabbit in Gialmi

A 3- to 4-pound rabbit
4 bay leaves
1 cup prosciutto, cut into ½-inch cubes
½ cup olive oil
1 cup dry white wine
1 teaspoon rosemary
6 cloves garlic, finely minced
Freshly ground black pepper to taste
Hot red-pepper flakes to taste (optional)

Cut rabbit into serving pieces as you would chicken. Arrange the rabbit pieces in a skillet and sprinkle with the remaining ingredients. Cover, and cook over medium heat until rabbit is tender, about 1¼ hours. Serve with broccoli or any winter vegetable. Serves 4 to 6.

CONIGLIO ALLA MARCHIGIANA
Rabbit Marchigiana

A 3-pound rabbit
1 cup dry white wine
½ cup olive oil
4 cloves garlic, finely chopped
1 tablespoon rosemary
Salt and freshly ground black pepper

Cut rabbit into serving pieces as you would chicken. Place rabbit pieces in one layer in a skillet. Do not add oil but cook the pieces, turning occasionally, until the external moisture on them evaporates. Begin with a low heat and increase heat as liquid is drawn out. Do not brown.

Add remaining ingredients, cover, and simmer over medium heat until rabbit is tender, about 45 minutes to 1 hour. Add a little more wine if the pan becomes too dry. Serves 4.

CONIGLIO ALLA CACCIATORA
Rabbit Hunter Style

A 3-pound rabbit
½ cup olive oil
3 whole cloves garlic
1 cup sliced mushrooms*
1 cup dry white wine
1 tablespoon rosemary
1 tablespoon sweet basil
Salt and freshly ground black pepper
Hot pepper flakes (optional)
1 cup peeled, seeded tomatoes

Cut rabbit into serving pieces as you would chicken. Place the rabbit pieces in one layer in a skillet. Do not add oil but cook the pieces, turning occasionally, until external moisture on them evaporates. Begin with low heat and increase heat as liquid is drawn out. Do not brown.

Add the oil and garlic and cook over medium heat until meat starts to brown. Add the mushrooms. When the mushrooms have cooked for about 5 minutes, add the wine, rosemary, basil, salt, pepper and pepper flakes. Cover and simmer about 5 to 10 minutes.

Meanwhile, simmer the tomatoes in a saucepan for 5 minutes. Add tomatoes to the rabbit, cover and cook until rabbit is tender, about 45 minutes. If sauce becomes too dry, add a touch of boiling water. Serves 4 to 6.

* In Italy and America wild mushrooms are traditionally used to make this dish.

CONIGLIO SELVAGGIO
Wild Rabbit

1 medium-to-large wild rabbit
1 cup wine vinegar
¾ ounce dried imported Italian mushrooms
3 tablespoons olive oil
2 whole cloves garlic, plus 1 teaspoon chopped garlic
4 tablespoons chopped pancetta or bacon
½ cup dry white or red wine
2 bay leaves
1 teaspoon rosemary
1 cup tomatoes, strained
½ cup beef or chicken stock
Salt and freshly ground black or hot pepper

Skin and clean rabbit, saving only the liver. Cover rabbit with cold water in a large pot and add vinegar. Soak for about 4 hours. Dry with paper towels and cut into serving pieces as you would chicken. Soak mushrooms in warm water for 15 minutes.

Heat olive oil in a heavy skillet. Add rabbit and whole garlic cloves. Cook rabbit over high heat without cover, stirring with a wooden spoon. As rabbit begins to turn color, lower heat to moderate, and add pancetta or bacon. Continue to cook, uncovered, and when rabbit begins to brown, add wine, bay leaves, rosemary, drained mushrooms and chopped garlic. Cover, lower heat and simmer, stirring occasionally until wine cooks out. Add tomatoes, stock, salt, pepper or hot pepper to taste. Cover and simmer 45 minutes to 1 hour or until rabbit is tender. Discard garlic. Serve hot to 4 to 6.

carni
Meats

Lisa

About

meats

We rarely ate beef when I was a child because it was expensive and because my parents preferred fish, poultry and veal.

My father would occasionally treat us—and especially himself—to a good steak but we rarely used other cuts of beef. We never even had meatballs in our pasta sauces because my father thought that it was degrading to use "chopped-up" poor-quality beef, disguised to hide its poorness. He only made chopped beef after the war, when he could afford to buy a good cut and chop it himself.

BISTECCA AL PESTO
Beefsteak with Pesto

2 slices top round steak, ½ inch thick
2 tablespoons olive oil
2 tablespoons butter
Salt and freshly ground black pepper
½ teaspoon oregano
Juice of ½ lemon
2 tablespoons pesto (see Pesto #2, page 218), diluted in 2 tablespoons warm water

Heat oil and butter together in a skillet. Add steaks and cook, uncovered, over a high heat, as rapidly as possible. Turn the meat constantly for 5 minutes. Add remaining ingredients and cook rapidly for 5 minutes more. Continue to turn meat as it cooks. Serves 2.

BISTECCA ALLA PIZZAIOLA
Beefsteak with Tomato and Garlic Sauce

3 pounds chuck steak, 1 inch thick
3 tablespoons olive oil
3 cups potato, peeled and cut into ¼-inch slices
Salt and freshly ground black pepper
1 cup sliced onion
1 teaspoon finely chopped garlic
1 tablespoon chopped parsley, Italian if possible
2 cups chopped tomato
1 teaspoon oregano

Preheat oven to 450°. Trim all excess fat from beef. Rub steak on each side with 1 tablespoon of the olive oil. Place it in a baking pan and arrange potatoes around it. Pour remaining oil and salt and pepper to taste over potatoes.

Spread onion, garlic, parsley, tomato and oregano over steak. Bake in oven, uncovered, for 20 to 30 minutes, depending on desired doneness. Serves 4 to 6.

Note: Excellent with baked spinach.

BRACCIOLI CON SALSA
Steak with Sauce

#1

3 slices top round or flank steak, about ¼ inch thick
2 tablespoons finely chopped parsley, Italian if possible
3 slices salami or prosciutto, chopped
2 tablespoons grated Parmesan or Romano cheese
Salt and freshly ground black pepper to taste
Butter

Sprinkle ingredients on each slice of meat. Dot with butter. Roll as you would a jelly roll and tie ends. Simmer in meat sauce (page 215) until tender.

#2

3 slices top round or flank steak, about ¼ inch thick
3 raw sausages, sliced or split
2 tablespoons chopped parsley, Italian if possible
1 clove garlic, finely chopped
Salt and freshly ground black pepper to taste
Butter

Sprinkle ingredients on meat. Dot with butter. Roll as you would a jelly roll and tie the ends. Simmer in meat sauce (page 215) until tender.

#3

3 slices top round or flank steak, about ¼ inch thick
3 hard-boiled eggs, shelled
2 tablespoons chopped parsley, Italian if possible
1 teaspoon basil
1 clove garlic, finely chopped
Salt and freshly ground black pepper to taste
Butter

Place one egg in the center of each piece of meat. Sprinkle with the rest of the ingredients. Dot with butter. Roll as you would a jelly roll and tie. Simmer in meat sauce (page 215) until tender.

BISTECCA ALLA FIORENTINA
Florentine Beefsteak

In this Italian method, the olive oil seals in the meat juices, and the water catches the fat. Thus, there is no smoke from burning fat and no splattering on the stove. I myself believe that the fat-laden smoke which coats

*the meat when it is charcoal-broiled is harmful as well
as dirty. Steaks and chops cooked by this method taste
better too.*

A 3-pound porterhouse steak
Olive oil
Salt and freshly ground black pepper to taste
2 lemons

Preheat broiler.

Place 1 inch of water in a shallow broiling pan or skillet and
put a grill over the pan. The grill should be at least ½ inch above
the water.

Rub the steak with olive oil, salt and pepper to taste. Broil
steak on both sides under high heat. As the meat browns, sprinkle
with lemon juice, a little at a time, turning often until the steak
is cooked to desired doneness. Serves 4.

POLPETTE CON CARCIOFI
Meatballs with Artichokes

1½ pounds lean ground chuck
6 tablespoons grated Parmesan cheese
2 eggs, lightly beaten
2 tablespoons finely chopped parsley, Italian if possible
1 teaspoon finely chopped garlic
Salt and freshly ground black pepper
1 tablespoon olive oil
6 slices prosciutto
6 slices mozzarella cheese, ¼ inch thick
6 whole artichoke hearts, canned

Preheat oven to 450°.

Mix together ground meat, grated cheese, eggs, parsley, garlic and salt and pepper to taste. Form 6 meatballs and flatten them
as you would to make a thick hamburger.

Pour olive oil in a baking dish and put the six meatballs in the dish. Place on each meatball 1 slice of prosciutto and 1 slice of mozzarella. Top with an artichoke heart, turned upside down and pressed down gently. Cover baking dish and bake ½ hour. Serves 6.

POLPETTE CON PISELLI
Meatballs with Peas

MEATBALLS

¾ pound lean ground chuck
¾ pound lean ground pork
1 cup bread crumbs
½ cup milk
¾ cup chopped onion
1 teaspoon thyme
½ cup dried raisins
½ cup grated Parmesan or Romano cheese
½ cup chopped parsley, Italian if possible
2 eggs, lightly beaten
Salt and freshly ground black pepper to taste
1 tablespoon olive oil
½ cup dry white wine

Soak bread crumbs in milk for 10 minutes, then squeeze out excess milk. In a large bowl, mix together all ingredients for the meatballs except the olive oil and wine.

Shape about 18 to 20 meatballs the size of golfballs. Coat a broiling tray with the olive oil and arrange meatballs on it. Broil under high heat, turning carefully with a spatula so that meatballs do not break. When they are golden brown on all sides, sprinkle with wine, cover, and lower heat. Cook for 5 minutes. Set aside and keep warm while you prepare the sauce.

SAUCE

1 cup chopped onion
3 tablespoons olive oil
1 clove garlic, finely chopped
1 teaspoon oregano
2 cups chopped, seeded tomatoes
Salt and freshly ground black pepper
2 cups green peas
½ cup chopped prosciutto

Preheat oven to 400°.

Sauté onions in olive oil. When onion wilts, add garlic. Simmer 3 to 4 minutes, then add oregano, tomatoes and salt and pepper to taste. Cover, and cook over low heat for 5 minutes.

Meanwhile, place green peas and prosciutto in a pot and cover with water. Cook gently, covered, until peas are tender. Drain and add to tomato mixture. Cover and simmer for about 5 minutes.

Place meatballs on a baking dish and pour pea-and-tomato sauce over them. Cover and bake 30 to 40 minutes. Serves 6.
Note: Excellent with mashed potatoes or rice.

POLPETTE DI RISO ALLA ROMANO
Meat-Stuffed Rice Balls Roman Style

¼ pound lean ground pork
¼ pound lean ground beef
3 tablespoons grated Parmesan cheese
½ teaspoon oregano
1 egg plus 4 eggs, separated
½ teaspoon minced garlic
Dash of nutmeg
Salt and freshly ground black pepper to taste
2 cups rice
4 tablespoons chopped parsley, Italian if possible
2 cups finely ground bread crumbs

Mix ground meat, cheese, oregano, 1 egg, garlic, nutmeg and salt and pepper together. Form meatballs about 1½ inch in diameter. Cook meatballs in a skillet with 1 tablespoon of olive oil over moderate heat, turning often until brown. Set aside.

In the meantime cook about 2 to 3 cups of marinara sauce (page 214) or meat sauce (page 215).

When the sauce is cooked, add meatballs, cover and simmer for 15 minutes.

Boil rice in salted water and cook until tender but firm, al dente. Drain rice and rinse in cold water. Mix rice well with parsley, egg yolks, salt and pepper. Form balls about the size of baseballs and force the smaller meatballs into the centers of the rice balls. Smooth out rice ball, adding more rice if necessary.

Hold ball in one hand. With your free hand spread egg white over ball, then cover with bread crumbs, shaping the ball as the crumbs are added. When the ball is firm and covered with bread crumbs, set aside. Repeat process to make 8 balls.

Put enough corn oil or peanut oil in a small skillet to fill it halfway. When oil is hot, pick up a ball with a slotted spoon and place it gently in the oil. When ball is a golden brown, turn. Remove from oil when brown on all sides. Place on a platter covered with paper towels and repeat process until all balls are cooked. To serve, place balls on another platter, pour hot sauce over them and sprinkle with grated cheese. Serve hot as a first or second course to 4.

Note: Mozzarella, cut into pieces the size of meatballs, may be substituted for meatballs.

INVOLTINI DI VITELLO
Veal Birds

5 slices veal scaloppine
2 slices prosciutto, chopped
Parmesan cheese
4 tablespoons butter
Sage, fresh or dried
Chopped parsley, Italian if possible
Salt and freshly ground black pepper
¼ cup imported Marsala

Sprinkle each slice of veal scaloppine with prosciutto, Parmesan cheese, dots of about ½ of the butter, sage, parsley and salt and pepper to taste. Roll up each scaloppine as you would a jelly roll and fasten ends with a toothpick or string.

Heat the remaining 2 tablespoons of butter in a skillet. When the butter is hot, add veal and sprinkle with salt and pepper. Cook, uncovered, over high heat, turning often. As soon as veal is lightly browned, add wine and continue to cook, uncovered, for 3 to 5 minutes, turning often. Serve hot to 3 to 4.

COSTOLETTI DI VITELLO CON BROCCOLI NERO
Veal Chops with Broccoli

6 to 7 loin veal chops
4 tablespoons olive oil
3 whole garlic cloves
Salt and freshly ground black pepper
½ cup dry white wine
1 cup coarsely chopped tomato
1 cup warm stock or water
1 bunch fresh broccoli, cleaned

Heat oil in a wide skillet. Add chops, garlic and salt and pepper to taste. Cook, uncovered, over high heat, turning meat often. When veal begins to brown, add wine. Cover and lower heat. Cook about 3 minutes, remove cover and turn up the heat. Simmer until wine cooks out. Discard garlic. Remove chops, set aside and keep warm.

In the meantime in a separate pot, cook tomatoes, uncovered, with stock or water, over medium-low heat for 10 minutes.

Blanch broccoli in boiling water. Drain and place in the fat in the same skillet used to cook the veal. Cover and simmer for several minutes. Add chops and tomatoes and simmer, uncovered, for 10 minutes. If there is too much liquid left in the pan, turn up the heat and reduce. Serves 6.

SPEZZATO DI VITELLO CON CARCIOFI
Veal Stew and Artichokes

4 tablespoons olive oil, or half oil and half butter
1 pound veal shoulder, cut into 1-inch cubes
4 fresh artichokes,* about the size of lemons, cut in quarters
3 garlic cloves
1 cup chopped onion
Salt and freshly ground black pepper
½ cup dry white wine
1 tablespoon rosemary
2 bay leaves
2 tablespoons chopped parsley, Italian if possible
1 cup roughly chopped tomato

Preheat oven to 400°. Heat oil in a skillet and add veal. Cook over high heat, stirring constantly. Remove tough outer leaves and tips of artichokes. Add artichokes, garlic, onions and salt and pepper to taste. When onion wilts, add wine and herbs. Cover and lower heat. Cook gently for about 5 minutes. Add tomato and cook 3 to 5 minutes more.

Put skillet in oven, cover and bake 15 to 20 minutes or until artichokes are tender. Discard garlic. Serves 6.

* These tiny artichokes are available in Italian markets. One box frozen artichoke hearts or one can artichoke hearts, drained, may be substituted.

SPEZZATO DI VITELLO CON CIPOLLE
Veal Stew with Onions

1 pound veal shoulder or leg, cut into 1-inch cubes
¼ cup olive oil
¼ cup wine vinegar
3 medium onions, sliced
2 tablespoons chopped parsley, Italian if possible
Salt and freshly ground black pepper

Heat oil in a skillet. Add veal and cook, uncovered, over high heat, stirring often. When veal begins to brown, add vinegar, cover, and lower heat.

Cook for several minutes, then turn up heat, remove cover and cook out the vinegar. Add onions, parsley and salt and pepper to taste. Turn heat to low, cover skillet and simmer gently until onion is cooked. Add a little stock or warm water if needed. Serves 4.

Note: Excellent with rice or boiled potatoes.

COSTOLETTE DI VITELLO CON PEPERONI
Veal Chops with Peppers

6 loin veal chops
3 sweet red peppers*
2 medium onions
½ cup olive oil
½ cup dry white wine
2 cups peeled tomatoes
Salt and freshly ground black pepper

Preheat oven to 400°.

Core the peppers, remove the seeds and cut into strips. Slice and separate onions into rings. Heat half the oil in a skillet and

* You *can* use green peppers, but the red look much better with this dish.

cook the pepper strips over high heat until they are tender. The skin side should look slightly scorched. Set them aside.

In an ovenproof skillet, heat the remaining oil and add the chops. Cook on both sides, turning frequently, until golden brown. Add the sliced onions and cook, stirring frequently, until they are limp. Add the wine and continue cooking until most of the wine evaporates. Add the tomatoes, salt and pepper to taste, and cook, stirring, until juices are slightly thickened. Add the peppers and bake in oven 10 to 15 minutes. Serves 6.

SPEZZATO DI VITELLO CON PATATE
Veal Stew with Potatoes

This is an excellent winter dish, though I have never tasted it anywhere outside my own home.

1¾ pounds veal shoulder or leg, cut into 1-inch cubes
3 medium potatoes
½ cup olive oil
2 whole garlic cloves
Salt and freshly ground black pepper
¼ cup dry white wine
1 teaspoon rosemary

Peel and cut potatoes into pieces about ¼ inch thick and 1 inch square. Soak in cold water for 15 minutes. Drain and dry with paper towels.

Heat half the oil in a skillet, and when it is hot, add veal and garlic. Cook, uncovered, over high heat, stirring often. Add salt and pepper to taste. When meat begins to brown, add wine and rosemary. Cover, lower heat and simmer 5 to 7 minutes.

Add potatoes and remaining olive oil. Cover, and cook over low heat. Stir often and add a little warm stock or warm water if needed to keep mixture moist. Cook until potatoes are tender. (Some potatoes will dissolve and some will stick to skillet.) Discard garlic. Serves 6 to 8.

SCALOPPINE DI VITELLO CON PISELLI
Veal Scaloppine with Peas

1 pound veal scaloppine, cut into 4-inch strips and as thin as possible
1 cup green peas
1 medium onion, finely chopped
4 tablespoons butter or half butter and half olive oil
1 cup chopped tomato
1 teaspoon dried basil or 1 tablespoon chopped fresh basil
Salt and freshly ground black pepper
Flour
½ cup imported Marsala
½ pound mozzarella cheese, sliced ½ inch thick
Grated Parmesan cheese

Cover peas with water and cook until they are almost tender. Drain and set aside.

In a separate pot, sauté onions in 2 tablespoons of the butter. When onion wilts, add tomato, basil and salt and pepper to taste. Cover, and simmer over low heat for 10 minutes. Then add peas and simmer for 5 minutes more. Set aside.

Dust the veal with flour. Heat remaining butter in a wide skillet. When the butter is hot, add veal and cook over high heat, turning constantly. As soon as veal colors, add wine and salt and pepper to taste. Continue tossing veal.

When wine thickens, after several minutes, turn off heat. Place a slice of mozzarella on each piece of veal and broil under high heat. When edges of mozzarella begin to brown, pour peas and tomatoes over it, sprinkle with Parmesan cheese and return to broiler for 2 to 3 minutes. Serve immediately to 4.

OSSO BUCCO
Veal Shanks

6 pieces veal shank, about 3 inches thick
Flour
3 tablespoons olive oil
2 whole garlic cloves
1 medium onion, finely chopped
½ cup chopped carrot
1 tablespoon basil
Salt and freshly ground black pepper
1 cup dry white wine
2 cups tomatoes, strained
2 tablespoons butter

Preheat oven to 400°.

Dredge veal with flour. Heat olive oil in a wide skillet. Add veal and cook, uncovered, over medium heat. Turn shanks when they begin to brown. Add garlic, and continue to simmer until brown on all sides. Add onion, carrot, basil, and salt and pepper to taste. When onion wilts, add wine, cover and lower heat. Simmer for 7 to 10 minutes, stirring often. Add tomatoes and butter. Cover again, and continue simmering for a few minutes longer.

Place skillet in oven and cook ½ hour. Then, lower heat to 350° and bake for 30 minutes. Meanwhile, prepare gremolada.

GREMOLADA

2 tablespoons chopped parsley, Italian if possible
1 clove garlic, chopped
1 teaspoon fresh or ½ teaspoon dried sage
1 lemon rind, grated

Mix together all ingredients and scatter over veal shanks. Return to oven and cook 10 more minutes. Serve with Risotto (page 64) or Cappelletti (page 42) to 4 to 6.

PETTO DI VITELLO RIPIENO AL MARSALA
Stuffed Veal Breast with Marsala

1 boned veal breast
1½ cups fresh ricotta
2 tablespoons chopped parsley, Italian if possible
3 tablespoons grated Parmesan cheese
1 egg, lightly beaten
¼ teaspoon nutmeg
¼ pound chopped boiled ham
Salt and freshly ground black pepper
2 tablespoons butter or olive oil
1 teaspoon rosemary
¾ cup imported Marsala

Preheat oven to 450°.

Mix together ricotta, parsley, Parmesan cheese, egg, nutmeg, boiled ham and salt and pepper to taste. Blend well. Lay veal flat and spread surface with stuffing, being careful not to place stuffing too close to edges of meat. Gently roll veal as you would a jelly roll. When the roll is complete, tie with string and sew the ends together.* Rub with salt, pepper and butter. Place veal roll in a baking pan. Sprinkle with rosemary and bake, uncovered, for about 1 hour, basting often. Add wine, cover and cook for 30 minutes. Continue to baste often.

Let the meat rest for at least 3 hours before serving. In fact, this dish is best served the day after it is cooked. Serve cold, cut into slices ½ inch thick. Serves 4.

* It is essential to sew the veal roll well enough so that when the ricotta expands it does not flow out.

PETTO DI VITELLO RIPIENO
Stuffed Breast of Veal

A breast of veal, with pocket, about 3½ pounds
½ pound lean ground chuck
3 eggs, lightly beaten
½ cup bread crumbs
3 tablespoons grated Parmesan or Romano cheese
1 clove garlic, finely chopped
2 tablespoons chopped parsley, Italian if possible
Salt and freshly ground black pepper
3 tablespoons olive oil
1 tablespoon rosemary
1 cup dry white wine
3 large potatoes, peeled and sliced lengthwise

Preheat oven to 400°.

Mix together thoroughly the ground chuck, eggs, bread crumbs, cheese, garlic, parsley and salt and pepper to taste. Blend well. Stuff pocket of veal breast with mixture and sew pocket together.

Rub veal with one tablespoon of the olive oil, rosemary and a little salt and pepper. Place in a baking pan and pour remaining oil over veal. Bake, uncovered, until veal begins to brown. Add wine, cover and baste often, adding stock or water if needed. Bake about 50 minutes, then add potatoes. Turn potatoes occasionally so that they do not stick to the pan. Cook about 20 minutes more or until potatoes are tender. Serves 6 to 8.

AGNELLO
About Lamb

My father used to buy a milk-fed baby lamb from a local farmer every Easter season. He would bring it home and keep it in the cellar, feeding it for four or five days. The lamb would become my pet, but I knew that my father was going to kill it, and somehow when the day came for the lamb to be slaughtered, I was able to detach myself from the animal I had been playing with and to think of it as food rather than as a companion. In fact, I would help my father by holding the lamb down during the slaughtering. It was less painful than it sounds because my father had been a farmer and knew how to kill an animal humanely and quickly. Like all poor children, I understood that we needed food—though, I must confess, I never ate much lamb as a child.

Interestingly, when I went to Italy years later, I noticed that the young people on my grandfather's farm had the same sort of attitude. They thought of animals as food, as the means of their own survival. This attitude differs a lot from our own violent society which cannot stand seeing a rabbit hanging in a market but which commits daily crimes of violence at home and abroad.

AGNELLO CON CARCIOFI
Lamb with Artichokes

1 pound lean lamb (leg if possible), cut into 1-inch cubes
5 fresh artichokes,° about the size of lemons
Juice of 1 lemon
2 tablespoons olive oil
Salt and freshly ground black pepper
1 whole garlic clove
1 onion, thinly sliced
2 bay leaves
¾ tablespoon rosemary
2 tablespoons butter
1 cup dry white wine
1 teaspoon dried mint or 2 teaspoons chopped fresh mint

° These tiny artichokes are available in Italian markets. Frozen or canned artichokes may be used. Add before placing meat in oven.

Preheat oven to 400°.

Remove tough leaves and cut fresh artichokes into wedges about ¼ inch thick. Soak in cold water and lemon juice for 15 minutes.

Drain and set aside. Heat olive oil in an ovenproof skillet and add lamb and salt and pepper to taste. Cook, uncovered, over high heat, stirring often. As meat colors, add garlic and onions. After 3 to 4 minutes, add artichoke wedges. Cover, and simmer over moderate heat for 5 minutes. Add bay leaves, rosemary and butter. Simmer until liquid evaporates, then add wine and mint. Cover, lower heat; stir occasionally and simmer for about 5 minutes. Place, covered, in oven and bake about 15 minutes or until artichokes are tender. Serves 4 to 6.

AGNELLO CON SALSA DI UOVA
Lamb with Egg Sauce

1 pound lean lamb shoulder or leg, cut into 1-inch pieces
Flour
½ cup diced pancetta or bacon
1 tablespoon olive oil
Salt and freshly ground black pepper
⅔ cup dry white wine
1 teaspoon rosemary
1 teaspoon fresh chopped sage or ½ teaspoon dried sage
½ cup chicken or beef stock
2 egg yolks
Juice of ½ lemon
1 tablespoon minced parsley, Italian if possible

Dust lamb with flour.

Sauté pancetta or bacon in olive oil. When pancetta begins to brown, add lamb and salt and pepper to taste. Turn up heat and cook, uncovered, until brown, stirring often. When lamb is brown, add wine, rosemary and sage. Cover, lower heat and cook for 5 minutes. Remove cover and cook several minutes more. Heat stock and add to lamb. Cover and cook over medium heat for about 15 minutes.

In the meantime, in a large bowl, mix egg yolks, lemon juice, parsley, and a little salt and pepper. Blend well. Add egg sauce to meat, mixing constantly for several minutes until eggs cook. Serve hot to 2 or 3.

Note: Excellent with rice or potatoes.

AGNELLO IMBOTTITO
Stuffed Lamb

3 pounds leg of lamb, boned
3 tablespoons olive oil
2 tablespoons chopped parsley, Italian if possible
1 clove garlic, minced
1 teaspoon chopped fresh sage or ½ teaspoon dried sage
2 tablespoons rosemary
10 cloves
1 tablespoon chopped lemon rind
Salt and freshly ground black pepper
3 thin slices prosciutto
½ cup wine vinegar
3 small onions, left whole
3 carrots, cut in half

Preheat oven to 425°.

Wash and dry lamb. Spread meat flat and rub with 1 tablespoon of the olive oil. Sprinkle with parsley, garlic, sage, 1 tablespoon of the rosemary, cloves, lemon rind and salt and pepper to taste. Lay prosciutto on top of the herbs. Roll lamb tight and tie as you would a roast. Rub the outside of lamb with 1 tablespoon of the olive oil, the remaining rosemary and a little salt and pepper. Add remaining olive oil to roasting pan if meat is quite lean. Roast meat, uncovered, basting often. When meat is brown, add vinegar, onions and carrots. Cover, and lower heat to 400°. Bake about 1 to 1¼ hours, basting often. Then remove meat from oven and allow to rest. Strain off fat from sauce, serve vegetables with lamb, pouring sauce over each portion. Serves 6.

AGNELLO IN AGRODOLCE
Sweet and Sour Lamb

1 pound lean lamb shoulder or leg, cubed
3 tablespoons olive oil
1 cup sliced onion
¼ cup wine vinegar
2 teaspoons sugar
½ tablespoon dried basil
Salt and freshly ground black pepper
2 tablespoons tomato paste
¼ cup milk

Heat oil in a skillet, then add lamb. Cook, uncovered, over high heat, turning often. When meat begins to brown, add onion. Lower heat to moderate and stir frequently.

Mix vinegar with sugar and when onion wilts, add to lamb. Cover and turn down heat to low. After 3 to 4 minutes, add basil and salt and pepper to taste. Cover and simmer until most of liquid evaporates.

Mix tomato paste and milk together until well blended. Then add to lamb. Cover and continue cooking over low heat, stirring often, for 15 minutes. Serve with rice to 3.

Note: Italian spring lamb is milk-fed, much smaller, more tender and less fat than American spring lamb. All lamb recipes should be made with this in mind.

AGNELLO ALLA FIORENTINA
Lamb Florentine Style

1 pound lean lamb shoulder or leg, cut into 1-inch cubes
2 tablespoons olive oil
1 teaspoon minced garlic
1 teaspoon rosemary
Salt and freshly ground black pepper
⅓ cup finely chopped prosciutto
½ cup tomatoes, strained
½ cup chicken or beef stock
1 cup green peas, parboiled

Heat oil in a skillet and add lamb. Cook, uncovered, over high heat. As lamb begins to brown, add garlic, rosemary and salt and pepper to taste. When garlic begins to brown, add prosciutto, and simmer over low heat, uncovered, for 3 to 4 minutes. Then add tomatoes and broth. Cover, and cook over high heat for about 10 minutes. Add peas, lower heat, and cook until peas are tender. Serve on mashed potatoes or rice to 3 or 4.

AGNELLO IN POTACCHIO ALLA MARCHIGIANA
Lamb Stew Marchigiana

3 pounds lamb shank, boned
2 whole garlic cloves
3 tablespoons olive oil
Salt and freshly ground black pepper
½ cup dry white wine
1 tablespoon rosemary
2 tablespoons chopped parsley, Italian if possible
1 cup chopped tomatoes
2 medium potatoes, thinly sliced
¼ cup beef or chicken stock or water

Preheat oven to 400°.

Remove fat, tendons, etc., from lamb and cut into pieces as you would meat for stew.

Cook garlic in olive oil in a wide skillet for several minutes, then discard garlic. Add lamb and salt and pepper to taste. Cook, uncovered, over high heat, stirring often. When lamb begins to brown, add wine, rosemary and parsley. Cover, lower heat and cook for 5 minutes. Then add tomatoes and simmer 3 to 5 minutes. Add potatoes and stock or water. Cover, and simmer several minutes more. Place stew in oven and bake for 45 minutes to 1 hour. Serves 6.

AGNELLO IN POTACCHIO
Lamb Shanks or Neck Bones with Vegetables

This dish can be made with all sorts of vegetables, such as white beans, squash and turnips.

4 lamb shanks or 8 neck bones*
4 tablespoons olive oil
Salt and freshly ground black pepper
8 small onions
4 whole garlic cloves
1 cup dry white wine
1 tablespoon rosemary
1 teaspoon thyme
1 teaspoon chopped fresh mint or ½ teaspoon dried mint
1½ pounds cabbage, cut in ½-inch chunks
4 carrots, cut in 1-inch pieces
2 stalks celery, chopped
1½ cups chopped green peppers
2 bay leaves
2 cups precooked green peas
3 medium potatoes, cut in large pieces

* The neck bones and shanks are economy cuts but are far tastier than most other parts of the lamb.

Preheat oven to 400°.

Remove excess fat from lamb. Place in a wide skillet, with 1 tablespoon of the olive oil. Add salt and pepper to taste and cook, uncovered, over moderate heat. As lamb begins to brown, add onions and garlic. When onions wilt, drain and discard all fat from pan.

Return skillet to heat and add wine, rosemary, thyme and mint. Cover, lower heat, and simmer 5 to 7 minutes.

In the meantime, boil cabbage in 4 cups of boiling water. Boil for 5 minutes, drain, but save 2 cups of liquid, and set cabbage aside. Place lamb and its juices in an ovenproof casserole. Add cabbage and the 2 cups of reserved water. Add all remaining ingredients except peas and potatoes.

Cover, place in oven, and cook for ½ hour. Add peas and potatoes and cook 45 minutes to 1 hour more. Taste for salt and pepper. Discard garlic and serve hot to 6 to 8.

SCALOPPINE DI MAIALE
Pork Scaloppine

2 tablespoons olive oil
¾ pound lean boneless pork tenderloin, cut into ¼-inch slices
2 cloves garlic, chopped
1 teaspoon rosemary
Salt and freshly ground black pepper to taste
Juice of ½ lemon

Heat oil in a wide skillet, add pork and all remaining ingredients except the lemon juice. Cook, uncovered, over high heat, turning pork pieces with a spatula so that they do not stick. When meat browns add lemon juice. Toss several times, and continue cooking for about 15 minutes. Serve hot with boiled or mashed potatoes to 4.

COSTOLETTE DI MAIALE IN SALSA PICCANTE
Pork Chops in a Piquant Sauce

An excellent winter dish.

1 tablespoon butter
6 pork chops, about ¾ inch thick
½ cup chopped onion
3 tablespoons wine vinegar
1 tablespoon flour
1 cup chicken or beef stock
2 tablespoons capers, drained
3 tablespoons chopped parsley, Italian if possible
Salt and freshly ground black pepper

Preheat oven to 450°.

Heat butter in a skillet large enough to hold chops. When butter melts, add chops and cook, uncovered, over high heat, turning chops often. When chops brown, turn heat to low, cover, and simmer about 15 minutes. Remove chops and discard most of the fat. Add onion to pan and cook several minutes in remaining fat. Turn up heat and add vinegar. Cook for a few minutes, then add flour. Mix well for a minute or less, then add stock, capers and parsley. Lower heat and simmer for several minutes. Pour off most of the sauce, return chops to pan and pour sauce over them. Add salt and pepper to taste, cover tightly, and bake in oven for about 15 minutes. Serve hot with boiled potatoes to 6.

ABOUT SAUSAGES

One of the most successful parties Ellie and I have ever had was a sausage-making party. I coarsely ground a pork butt and put the meat in a bowl surrounded by other bowls filled with various ingredients for sausage. When our friends arrived, we all stood together making sausages, some people tying, some stuffing. Then I showed our guests how to prepare sausage with cauliflower, with peppers, and broiled alone. I think that I produced several sausage-makers that day.

My own children, especially Gina, love to stuff sausage and to eat them—though for the children I leave out the pepper.

SALSICCIE CON SEME DI FINOCCHI
Pork Sausage with Fennel Seeds

2 to 4 strands pork casings*
3 pounds boneless pork butt
1½ teaspoons salt
2 tablespoons freshly ground black pepper
1½ teaspoons crushed fennel seeds
Hot-pepper flakes or cayenne pepper to taste (optional)

* Available in Italian stores.

Rinse pork casings well and let them soak in cold water at least 1 hour. Rinse well and drain thoroughly.

Remove most of the fat from pork butt. Place meat on a flat surface, slice it thinly, then chop coarsely (this method is preferable, although it may be coarsely ground in a meat grinder).

Blend meat with salt, pepper, fennel seeds and pepper flakes. Stuff one casing at a time. To do this, slip one end of the casing over the mouth of a funnel with a big spout—or use a regular sausage stuffer. Use finger to push the casing down the spout or over the mouth of the sausage stuffer. Tie the end of the casing with string. Place funnel in an upright position and start adding meat, pushing it through the funnel and into the casing, letting the casing slip away gradually as it is filled. Tie the sausage-filled casings every 3 inches to make links. If there are air bubbles, prick the sausage with a needle to let the air escape. The sausage may be broiled or fried in the usual manner. Yield: 3 pounds of sausage.

SALSICCIE DI FEGATO DI MAIALE AI FERRI
Broiled Pork-Liver Sausage

4 pork-liver sausages
Enough caul * to cover sausages
4 bay leaves
1 lemon

Place two pairs of sausages beside each other on a piece of caul large enough to wrap them in. Alternate bay leaves with sausages. Fold the caul over the sausages and bay leaves, and tie with a string as you would a roll of meat. Cook over hot coals or under a broiler, squeezing lemon juice over sausages as they brown. When cooked, in about 10 minutes, remove from heat and discard caul. Serves 2.

* Available in Italian stores.

SALSICCIE DI FEGATO DI MAIALE
Pork-Liver Sausages

I got this recipe from my grandfather when I visited him in Centobuchi. The liver must be absolutely fresh. My grandfather would give me enough to fill my suitcase when I went back to Florence to study.

2 to 4 strands of pork casings*
2 pounds pork liver
¾ cup pork caul * or fat, chopped
¾ cup chopped orange rind
2 cloves garlic, chopped
Salt and freshly ground black or hot pepper to taste
Lemon juice

Discard tough membranes of the liver. Chop liver coarsely, then mix it together with all the ingredients, except the pork casings.

Prepare casings and stuff them as on page 163 to make 12 sausages, each about 3½ inches long.

Sauté liver sausages in enough olive oil to coat the bottom of the skillet.

Cook, uncovered, over medium heat until sausages are cooked, about 10 to 15 minutes. Squeeze lemon juice over sausages 2 minutes before serving. Do not overcook; the center of sausage should not be too dry. Serves 6.

* Available in Italian food stores.

SALSICCIE CON FAGIOLI
Sausages with Beans

SAUSAGES

8 Italian-sausage links
2 tablespoons olive oil or pork fat
½ cup dry white wine

Sauté sausages in oil, over moderate heat, turning occasionally. When sausages are brown, add wine, cover and lower heat. Cook for about 5 minutes. Remove cover, turn up heat and cook out wine. Set sausages aside and keep warm. Reserve pan juices.

BEANS

1 cup chopped onion
1 cup chopped celery
3 tablespoons olive oil
1 teaspoon rosemary
2 bay leaves
2 cloves garlic, chopped
1 cup chopped, seeded tomatoes
1 can cannellini beans,* drained
Salt and freshly ground black pepper

Preheat oven to 375°.
In an ovenproof casserole, sauté onion and celery in olive oil. Simmer, covered, for about 10 minutes or until onion wilts. Then add herbs, tomatoes, beans and salt and pepper to taste. Cook, covered, for 5 minutes. Add sausages and 3 tablespoons of reserved pan juices. Cover and bake for 20 to 30 minutes. Serve hot to 4.

* You can use 1 cup dried white beans, soaked overnight, and cooked in water until tender.

SALSICCIE ALLA SICILIANA
Pork Sausages Sicilian Style

2 to 4 strands of pork casings*
½ pound pork butt, coarsely ground
½ cup chopped provolone cheese
3 tablespoons chopped parsley, Italian if possible
½ teaspoon fennel seeds
½ cup dry white wine
1 teaspoon salt
1 teaspoon crushed black pepper
4 tablespoons olive oil

Mix together all ingredients except pork casings and oil. Prepare and stuff casings (page 163). Place sausages in a skillet with olive oil and simmer, uncovered, over low heat until cooked. Serve hot to 4.

    * Available in Italian food stores.

SALSICCIE ALLA MARCHIGIANA
Italian Sausages Marchigiana

9 sweet or hot Italian-sausage links, or a combination of both (about 1½ pounds)
1 large cauliflower, broken into flowerets
2 tablespoons olive oil
2 onions, thinly sliced
1 tablespoon crushed fennel seeds
1 tablespoon chopped fresh basil or 1 teaspoon dried basil
1 teaspoon finely chopped fresh rosemary or ½ teaspoon dried rosemary
½ teaspoon chopped hot-pepper flakes
2 cloves garlic, finely minced
½ cup red wine vinegar
1 tablespoon tomato paste
½ cup warm water

Cook the sausages in a skillet, turning frequently, until brown and cooked through. Cook the cauliflower in boiling salted water for one minute. Drain. Remove the sausages and cut into 1-inch lengths. Set aside. Pour off most of the fat from the skillet and add the olive oil and cauliflower. Cook, shaking the skillet, until cauliflower is lightly browned. Add more oil if necessary. Add the onions and cook, stirring, until they are wilted. Add the fennel seeds, and the rosemary, pepper flakes, garlic and vinegar. Cook over low heat, stirring to blend, about 5 minutes. Dilute the tomato paste in the warm water and add it to sausages. Cover and simmer until cauliflower is barely tender, 5 to 10 minutes. Serve hot to 6.

SALSICCIE CON CAVOLO
Sausage with Savoy Cabbage

1 small head Savoy cabbage
¼ cup olive oil
6 links pork sausage with fennel seeds (page 162)
Salt and freshly ground black pepper
2 cloves garlic, finely chopped

Rinse cabbage head and drain. Cut into segments 1½ to 2 inches thick. Blanch in boiling water. Drain and set aside.

Heat half the oil in a skillet and add sausage. Cook, turning as necessary, until golden brown and cooked through. Drain and set aside. Blanch cabbage in boiling water; drain.

Heat remaining oil in a casserole and add cabbage, salt and pepper to taste and garlic. Cover tightly and simmer about 15 minutes. It is not necessary to add water unless cabbage starts to stick or burn, in which case add just enough boiling water to keep it from sticking. Stir occasionally.

Add sausage to cabbage and cover. Cook until cabbage is tender, 15 minutes or longer. Serves 4 to 6.

SPIEDINI DI FEGATO DI MAIALE ALLA RETICELLA
Pork Liver Wrapped in Caul

½ pound fresh pork liver, cut into 1½-inch cubes
1 tablespoon crushed rosemary
2 cloves garlic, sliced
Juice of 1 lemon
Salt and freshly ground black pepper
Caul
Bay leaves

Mix together rosemary, garlic, lemon juice, and salt and pepper to taste and marinate liver in this mixture for ½ hour.

Remove liver from marinade and wrap each cube, together with a bay leaf, in a piece of caul. Then spear the wrapped pieces onto skewers until all the liver is used. Broil over hot coals or under flame, basting occasionally with the marinade. Do not overcook. Liver should be pink inside. Serves 2.

'NDOCCA 'NDOCCA
(A provincial specialty from Abruzzi)

I don't know why the pork in this recipe is soaked for 6 hours, except that the original recipe called for either salted pork or very fresh pork. This recipe was sent to me by my cousin who lives in Abruzzi.

2 pig's feet, cut into 2-inch pieces
4 pork spareribs, cut into 2-inch pieces
6 cups assorted pig's parts (ears, jowls, etc.), cut into 1-inch cubes
2 cloves garlic, finely chopped
4 bay leaves
1 tablespoon rosemary
Salt and hot-pepper flakes
¼ cup crushed tomato

Soak the pork pieces in cold water to cover for 6 hours, changing the water occasionally. Drain the pork and put it in a pot (preferably earthenware) large enough to hold the pork covered with water and the remaining ingredients as they are added. Cover the pork with cold water and add the garlic, bay leaves, rosemary and salt and pepper flakes to taste. Cover and simmer 1½ hours. Add the tomato and cook 1 hour longer. Serve with boiled potatoes, cabbage or rice to 6.

ANIMELLE AL MARSALA
Sweetbreads with Marsala

1 pair sweetbreads
1½ cups beef stock
2 tablespoons butter
2 cloves garlic, minced
½ cup imported dry Marsala
1 teaspoon dried basil
Salt and freshly ground black pepper to taste

Soak sweetbreads in cold water for 1 hour. Drain, and cook whole sweetbreads in boiling stock for 10 minutes. Remove from stock and cool. (Save stock for future use.) Trim off all connective tissues and excess fat. With a sharp knife cut sweetbreads into slices about ¾ inch thick.

Heat butter in a skillet. Add sweetbreads and sauté, uncovered, over moderate heat. Turn, and as soon as sweetbreads begin to brown, add the rest of the ingredients. Simmer, uncovered, until wine cooks out. Serve very hot, with a fresh green vegetable, to 4.

ANIMELLE CON PISELLI
Sweetbreads with Peas

1 pair sweetbreads
1½ cups beef stock
2 cups green peas, precooked, or 1 can peas, drained
Flour
3 tablespoons butter
½ cup chopped tomatoes
1 tablespoon minced parsley, Italian if possible
1 teaspoon dried basil
Salt and freshly ground black pepper
1 small onion, chopped
½ cup imported dry Marsala
Grated Parmesan or Romano cheese

Soak sweetbreads in cold water for 1 hour. Drain and cook in boiling stock for 10 minutes. Remove from stock and cool. (Save stock for future use.) Trim off all connective tissues and excess fat. With a sharp knife cut sweetbreads into slices about ½ inch thick. Dust sweetbreads with flour. Set aside.

In the meantime, in a separate pot, place peas, 1 tablespoon of the butter, tomatoes, parsley, basil and salt and pepper to taste. Cover and simmer for 10 minutes. Set aside. In a skillet, heat remaining butter and sauté onion. When onion wilts, add sweetbreads and turn up heat to high. Cook, turning often, until edges of sweetbreads begin to brown. Add wine and continue to cook, uncovered, over high heat until most of the wine cooks out. Add peas-and-tomato mixture. Cover, lower heat, and simmer for 10 minutes. Serve hot, with grated cheese if you like, to 4.

ANIMELLE AL PESTO
Sweetbreads with Pesto

1 pair sweetbreads
2 tablespoons butter
1 small onion, chopped
½ cup imported dry Marsala
1 teaspoon thyme
Salt and freshly ground black pepper
2 tablespoons pesto (Pesto #1, page 217)

Soak sweetbreads in cold water for 1 hour. Drain and cook in boiling stock for 10 minutes. Remove from stock and cool. (Save stock for future use.) Trim off all connective tissues and excess fat. With a sharp knife cut sweetbreads into slices about ¾-inch thick.

Heat butter in a skillet. Add onion and sauté, uncovered, until onion wilts. Add sweetbreads, continue cooking, and when edges begin to brown, add wine, thyme and salt and pepper to taste. Turn up heat and cook over high heat, uncovered, stirring often for several minutes. As sauce begins to thicken, add pesto. Lower heat and simmer for about 3 minutes. Serve immediately to 2 or 3.

FEGATINI DI POLLO CON ASPARAGI
Chicken Livers with Fresh Asparagus

1 pound fresh asparagus
3 tablespoons olive oil or half oil and half butter
1 cup chopped scallion
2 cloves garlic, minced
1 pound chicken livers
1 teaspoon thyme
Salt and freshly ground black pepper to taste
½ cup dry white wine

Cut off and discard tough ends of asparagus and cut spears into 3-inch lengths. If spears are more than ½ inch thick, cut in half lengthwise. Sauté asparagus in oil over moderate heat, uncovered, in a wide skillet. When asparagus is tender, add all ingredients except the wine. Toss constantly as soon as livers take on color. Add wine, continue to toss and cook, uncovered, over moderate to high heat until livers are cooked. Do not overcook —livers should be pink inside. Serve immediately to 4.

FRITTELLE DI POLLO E CERVELLA
Chicken and Calves-Brains Fritters

1 cup cooked calves brains
2 cups diced boiled chicken
1 cup diced prosciutto
¾ cup grated Parmesan cheese or diced provolone
3 tablespoons minced parsley, Italian if possible
Salt and freshly ground black pepper to taste
Flour
Corn or peanut oil for deep frying

Soak brains 5 to 10 minutes in cold running water. Cover brains with water and cook for 5 minutes. Drain and allow to cool. Then remove and discard membrane.

Chop brains and place in a bowl with all ingredients, except the flour and oil. Mix well.

Roll mixture into balls about 1 to 1½ inch in diameter. Then roll the balls in flour. Let them rest several minutes, then roll them in flour again. Heat about 1 inch of peanut or corn oil in a skillet until very hot, and deep-fry balls until golden brown. Blot with paper towels and serve hot with lemon wedges to 4 to 6. Yields 20 to 25 balls.

Note: This dish is excellent as a hot antipasto or as a first or second course.

FEGATO ALLA GENOVESE
Calves Liver Genoese Style

3 tablespoons olive oil or butter
2 slices calves liver, about ¾ inch thick
½ medium onion, chopped
1 teaspoon rosemary
Salt and freshly ground black pepper
½ cup dry white wine
1 tablespoon pesto (Pesto #1, page 217)

Heat oil or butter in a skillet. Add liver and onion. Turn liver almost immediately and cook, uncovered, over high heat. Add rosemary, salt and pepper to taste. Turn liver often.

Cook for about 5 minutes and lower heat to medium. Continue to cook for about 3 minutes. Add wine, turn up heat and cook out wine. Add pesto diluted in 2 tablespoons water. Cook a few minutes more, turning liver. Do not overcook. Serve immediately to 2.

FEGATINI DI POLLO ALLA PRIMAVERA
Chicken Livers Primavera

1 pound chicken livers
¼ cup olive oil or half butter and half oil
2 medium onions, finely chopped
½ cup peeled, seeded, chopped ripe tomato
¼ cup chopped parsley, Italian if possible
¼ cup chopped scallion
1 teaspoon dried oregano
1 tablespoon chopped fresh basil or 1 teaspoon dried basil
1 cup dry white wine
Salt and freshly ground black pepper to taste

Pick over the chicken livers and remove tough membranes. Cut each liver into 2 parts.

Heat the oil or butter and oil in a skillet and add the onion. Cook, stirring, until onion wilts. Then add the tomato. Simmer until slightly thickened and add the livers. Cook over high heat, turning the livers occasionally, until they lose their red color. Add the remaining ingredients and simmer, partially covered, 4 to 5 minutes. Do not overcook—the livers should remain slightly pink inside. Serve with rice or mashed potatoes to 4.

ROGNONCINI DI VITELLO AI FERRI
Broiled Veal Kidney

2 veal kidneys
Olive oil
¼ teaspoon thyme
½ teaspoon rosemary
1 clove garlic, sliced
Salt and freshly ground black pepper
2 slices pancetta or bacon, cut in half
Juice of ½ lemon

Split kidneys in half and, with the point of a sharp knife, remove fat and veins from center of kidneys. Soak in salted water for 1 hour; rinse and drain.

Rub kidneys with olive oil. Place in a baking dish, side by side, and sprinkle with thyme, rosemary, garlic, and salt and pepper to taste. Lay pancetta or bacon on kidneys and broil under a high heat. After the bacon becomes crisp, add lemon juice. Do not overcook—kidneys should not be dry. Serves 2.

Note: Excellent with fresh green vegetables and salad.

ROGNONCINI DI VITELLO CON PISELLI
Veal Kidneys with Peas

4 veal kidneys
2 tablespoons olive oil
2 tablespoons butter
1 teaspoon rosemary
¼ cup chopped onion
Salt and freshly ground black pepper
½ cup dry red wine
1 teaspoon oregano
¼ cup chopped tomato
1 cup cooked green peas or 1 cup canned peas, drained

Split kidneys in half and, with the point of a sharp knife, remove fat and veins from center of kidneys. Soak in salted water for 1 hour; drain. Then cut into 1½-inch cubes. Heat oil and butter in a large skillet. When the oil is hot, add kidneys. Cook, uncovered, over high heat, stirring often with a wooden spoon. When liquid cooks out and kidneys begin to brown, add rosemary, onion and salt and pepper to taste. When onion wilts, add wine and oregano. Cover and lower heat. Simmer for 3 or 4 minutes, then remove cover and turn up heat for wine to evaporate. After most of the wine is cooked out, add tomato, cover, and simmer for 3 to 4 minutes. Then add peas, cover, and simmer for 10 minutes. Serve hot on rice to 6.

SALSICCIE CON ROGNONCINI DI VITELLO
Sausages and Veal Kidneys

4 tablespoons olive oil
4 links Italian sweet pork sausage
3 veal kidneys
2 large onions, chopped
3 whole garlic cloves
1 cup dry white wine
1 teaspoon basil
½ cup chopped scallion
1 teaspoon rosemary
Salt and freshly ground black pepper
1 cup chopped, seeded tomatoes

Heat 2 tablespoons of the oil in a wide skillet. Add sausages and sauté, uncovered, turning often. When sausages are cooked, cut into slices about ½ inch thick and set aside.

Split kidneys in half and, with the point of a sharp knife, remove fat and veins from center of kidneys. Then cut into 1½-inch cubes.

Pour off half the fat from the skillet and add kidneys. Cook, uncovered, over moderate heat, turning often. When kidneys begin to brown, add sausages and simmer together for 3 or 4 minutes.

Add remaining olive oil, onion and garlic. When onion wilts, add wine, basil, scallion, rosemary, and salt and pepper to taste. Cover, lower heat and simmer for 5 minutes. Remove cover, turn up heat and cook out the wine. Add tomatoes and cover. Simmer for about 10 minutes until tomatoes thicken. Remove garlic. Serves 4 to 6.

TRIPPA CON BROCCOLI
Tripe with Broccoli

1½ pounds honeycomb tripe
½ cup olive oil
1 medium onion, chopped
2 cloves garlic, minced
½ cup dry white wine
1 tablespoon basil
2 tablespoons minced parsley, Italian if possible
Salt and freshly ground black pepper
1¾ cups chopped, seeded tomatoes
2 tablespoons tomato paste
1 bunch broccoli
Grated Parmesan or Sardo cheese

Soak tripe in salted cold water for 1 hour; drain. With a sharp knife, remove all excess fat from smooth side of tripe. Cut tripe into strips ¼ inch wide and about 2 inches long. Wipe dry with paper towels. Put half of the olive oil in a wide pot and heat. When oil is hot, add tripe and cook, without cover, over high heat, turning often until liquid evaporates. Add onion and garlic. Lower heat and cook for 3 to 4 minutes. Add wine, basil, parsley and salt and pepper to taste. Cover and simmer for about 5 minutes.

Preheat oven to 450°.

Place tomatoes and tomato paste in a separate ovenproof casserole over high heat. When tomatoes come to a boil, add tripe mixture. Cover casserole and place in oven. Bake for 10 minutes, then lower oven to 400° and bake about 1 hour.

Clean broccoli and blanch in boiling water. Drain and add broccoli to tripe. Lower heat to 350°, add rest of olive oil and cook 15 to 20 minutes more. Serve hot, with or without rice, with grated cheese, to 6.

Note: The less olive oil cooks, the sweeter it is.

SUFRITTO #1
Veal Lung (and Heart) #1

1½ pounds veal lung and heart
½ cup olive oil
Salt and hot pepper
½ cup dry white wine
3 small onions, sliced
2 cloves garlic, minced
2 cups chopped, seeded tomatoes
¼ cup water
1 teaspoon oregano

Soak meat in salted cold water for 1 hour. Then cook meat in boiling water for 5 minutes, drain and dry with paper towels. With a sharp knife, remove nerves, fat, etc. Dice meat into pieces about ½ inch to ¾ inch square.

Heat oil in a wide skillet and add meat. Cook over high heat, without cover, stirring often with a wooden spoon. After several minutes add salt and hot pepper to taste. As meat begins to brown, lower heat to medium. When meat edges brown, add wine. Lower heat, cover and simmer for 3 to 4 minutes. Add onions and garlic and simmer another 3 to 4 minutes.

In the meantime, in a separate pot, bring tomatoes and water to a boil; add to meat. Add oregano, cover and simmer about 30 minutes. Serves 6 to 8.

SUFRITTO #2
Lung #2

1 pound lungs of spring lamb or kid
6 tablespoons olive oil
1 cup chopped onion
½ cup dry white wine
1 teaspoon oregano
1 tablespoon basil
Salt and hot pepper
2 cups seeded, chopped tomatoes

Soak lungs in salted cold water for 1 hour, drain and dry with a towel. Cut meat into pieces about ¾ inch square. Remove and discard all fat, veins, etc. Heat half of the oil in a skillet. Add lungs and turn up heat, stirring often with a wooden spoon. As meat begins to brown, add onion. When onion wilts, add wine, oregano, basil, and salt and pepper to taste. Cover and lower heat, simmering for 5 minutes. Remove cover, turn up heat and cook out wine. Add tomatoes and remaining olive oil, cover and simmer over moderate heat for 45 minutes to 1 hour. Sauce should be rather thick. Serves 2 to 4.

verdura

Vegetables

Lisa Giobbi

About

VeGeTaBLes

My father had been a farmer in Italy, and from the time he came to America, he always had a garden.

He once bought a plot of land on a very high hill, about a mile and a half from the house we rented in Waterbury, Connecticut. He dreamed of building a house on that lot, but he never did. In fact, he never got beyond digging a big hole, the beginning of a cellar. That hole ended up as the zucchini-and-cucumber bed.

Every evening, when he came home from work in the brass mills, he would trudge up the hill to his piece of land to work in his garden. I would go with him, and I had my own little corner to plant. My father planted great quantities of tomatoes and my mother would can enough of them to last us for the entire year.

He also planted peppers, cabbage, Italian pole beans, beets, squash, etc. When it was time to harvest the vegetables I would fill a basket and he would fill a bushel and we would carry the vegetables home.

When Ellie and I bought our place in Katonah, the first thing my father did on his very first visit to us was to look for a suitable place for a garden. He found a perfect spot and immediately began to turn over the soil. He took care of the garden for us until he died four years ago. A year before he died, he planted three peach trees in the garden with shoots he had started the year before from pits. After he planted the trees I asked Pop why in the world he had gone to the trouble to plant the trees in the middle of the garden, and he answered, "Because you won't have time to work on the garden after I die. This way at least you will have fresh peaches."

After my father died I was determined to keep up the garden, almost as a tribute to him. He always thought a tomato plant more beautiful than a flower. As I worked, to my surprise, everything I had watched him do and everything he taught me came back to me. I have had a wonderful garden ever since. My Italian pole beans are from seeds he gave me and I continue to dry my own seeds each year. I canned a hundred quarts of tomatoes from my garden last summer— tomatoes grown organically without pesticides. I plant a garden even if I go away for the summer and when I return there are always enough vegetables left to justify the effort.

To me, gardening is a ritual that all men should experience. Getting on your knees, turning the soil, and smelling the fresh earth is an experience that reminds men of their origins. It is extremely rewarding. It is also a great way to beat the system. Nothing is more satisfying than planting a seed, watching it grow, and then reaping the fruits of your labor. The final blessing is to cook your harvest and to nourish your own body and the bodies of those you love.

As a painter, I find gardening a necessary part of my creative experience. When my painting is going slowly, I work in the garden. More often than not, after a few hours of outside work, I return to my studio and see the problems before me in a different light. Painting is very much like growing things. When you plant a seed, all of the energies of the seed are directed toward reproducing so that the species survives. The mature plant drops its foliage and fertilizes the seed.

To me, painting is very much the same process: planting a seed for the next painting to grow from. The most important lesson the artist learns is to destroy his facility and his mannerisms, to enable him to fertilize, as in nature, the seed which must survive. When an artist stops planting seeds, he stops creating. Then he lives off his facility and becomes a hack by repeating himself over and over. Picasso is a great example of an artist who has not stopped planting seeds. You might call him the Johnny Appleseed of the contemporary art world. Hans Hoffman is another example of an artist who never stopped planting seeds.

When I moved to the country and started a garden, to my delight, gardening explained some situations I had instinctively felt about my painting but was not capable of defining intellectually. I feel cooking does not only involve filling your stomach but is part of the whole life scheme, and the involvement begins, like painting, with a seed—which is, after all, what life is all about.

CARCIOFI CON PISELLI
Artichokes with Fresh Peas

1½ cups green peas
6 fresh artichokes,* about the size of lemons
3 tablespoons olive oil
3 tablespoons butter
4 tablespoons diced prosciutto
Salt and freshly ground black pepper
2 tablespoons chopped parsley, Italian if possible

Place peas in saucepan, cover with water and cook until tender, about 5 minutes. Drain but save about ½ cup of the cooking liquid.

Remove and discard tough outer leaves and cut off artichoke tips. Cut artichokes in quarters and soak in cold water for 10 to 15 minutes. Drain and dry. Simmer artichokes in oil and butter for 5 minutes, stirring often. Add prosciutto and simmer for 2 more minutes. Add peas and reserved cooking liquid to artichokes. Add salt and pepper to taste and parsley. Cover and simmer until artichokes are tender, adding more water if necessary. Serves 6 to 8.

* Frozen artichoke hearts may be used if fresh are not available.

CARCIOFI RIPIENI DI CARNE
Artichokes Stuffed with Meat

8 artichokes, about the size of large lemons
6 tablespoons ground meat, half lean chuck, half lean pork
6 slices chopped salami or prosciutto
1 egg, lightly beaten
2 tablespoons Parmesan cheese
1 teaspoon chopped parsley, Italian if possible
Salt and freshly ground black pepper
2 cloves garlic
½ cup dry white wine
4 tablespoons olive oil

Preheat oven to 400°.

Clean artichokes by discarding tough outer leaves and snipping off tips. Cut off the stems, peel and set them aside. Force the center of each artichoke open to form a little well. Soak them in cold water, with the stems, for about 10 minutes. Drain and set aside.

In the meantime, make stuffing by mixing ground meat, salami, egg, cheese, parsley and salt and pepper to taste. Put a sliver of garlic in the leaves of each artichoke.

Place artichokes very snugly in a baking dish and force the stems between them. Stuff artichokes with stuffing. Pour wine and olive oil over artichokes. Cover pan tightly and bake until tender, about 1 hour. Add stock, warm water or more wine if liquid cooks out. Serves 8 as a vegetable, or 4 as a main course.

ASPARAGI AL FORNO
Baked Fresh Asparagus

1 bunch or about 1¼ pounds fresh asparagus
3 tablespoons dried mint or parsley
4 tablespoons olive oil or half oil and half butter
Salt and freshly ground black pepper to taste

Preheat oven to 400°. Wash and drain asparagus. Place asparagus spears closely in a baking pan and sprinkle remaining ingredients over them. Cover pan with foil and bake until asparagus is tender but firm to the bite, al dente, about 15 minutes. Serve hot to 4 to 6.

ASPARAGI IN PADELLA
Fried Asparagus

1 pound fresh asparagus
3 tablespoons olive oil or half butter and half oil
1 tablespoon chopped parsley, Italian if possible
Salt and freshly ground black pepper

Discard tough ends of asparagus, then wash and cut spears in 3-inch lengths. Put all ingredients in a skillet and cook, uncovered, over medium heat. As asparagus begins to brown, cover, lower heat and simmer until tender. Serves 4 to 6.
Note: You may sauté scallions (cut in quarters, lengthwise, and with roots trimmed and discarded) together with the asparagus for a very pretty dish.

FAGIOLI SECCHI ALLA FIORENTINA
Dried Beans Florentine Style

1 cup dried white beans
3 cups water
½ teaspoon dried sage or 2 or 3 fresh leaves
2 whole garlic cloves
1½ tablespoons olive oil
Salt and freshly ground black pepper to taste

Cover beans with water and soak overnight. Drain beans, then put all ingredients in a deep pot. Cover and boil gently for

1 hour. Continue to boil gently, with pot partially covered, until beans are tender. There should be very little liquid left when beans are cooked. If too much remains, turn up heat and reduce liquid. If there is not enough liquid to finish the cooking, add some warm water. Serves 4.

Note: Although the recipe does not call for tomatoes, I sometimes add a teaspoon of tomato paste or ¼ cup fresh tomatoes.

FAGIOLINI CON PATATE E ZUCCHINI #1
Green Beans with Potatoes and Zucchini #1

1 pound green beans*
1 medium potato, peeled and thinly sliced
2 small zucchini, cut in ½-inch slices
1 tablespoon chopped parsley, Italian if possible
½ cup olive oil
½ cup tomatoes, chopped
1 medium onion, sliced
1 tablespoon dried basil
¼ cup water
Salt and freshly ground black pepper to taste

Remove tips and break beans in half. Blanch beans and potatoes in boiling water. When water returns to a boil, remove vegetables and drain well. Mix vegetables with remaining ingredients in a wide skillet. Cover and cook over low heat until green beans are tender, about 15 to 20 minutes. Serves 6.

* Italian pole beans are best if available.

FAGIOLINI CON PATATE E ZUCCHINI #2
Green Beans with Potatoes and Zucchini #2

1 pound green beans
1 zucchini
1 large potato
½ cup olive oil
2 cloves garlic, finely chopped
1 teaspoon rosemary
Salt and freshly ground black pepper to taste

Slice green beans in half lengthwise and blanch in boiling water. Drain and save 1 cup of the cooking liquid. Cut zucchini into ½-inch slices and thinly slice the potato.

Sauté remaining ingredients in olive oil for 3 to 5 minutes. Add green beans, the reserved liquid, zucchini and potato. Cover and simmer over low heat until vegetables are tender. Serves 6.

FAGIOLINI CON PATATE E POMODORI
Fresh Italian Pole Beans with Tomatoes and Potatoes

This dish is best in the summertime when all ingredients are fresh.

1½ pounds fresh pole beans*
3 medium potatoes
6 tablespoons olive oil
2 cloves garlic, finely chopped
2 cups coarsely chopped tomatoes
2 tablespoons chopped fresh basil or 1 tablespoon dried basil
1 teaspoon chopped fresh mint or ½ teaspoon dried mint
2 tablespoons chopped parsley, Italian if possible
Salt and freshly ground black pepper
   * Fresh green beans may also be used.

Snap off ends and break beans in half. Peel potatoes and cut into cubes. Soak beans and potatoes in cold water for 15 minutes. In a wide pot or a skillet, put olive oil, garlic, tomatoes, basil, mint, parsley and salt and pepper to taste. Cover, and cook over low heat for 5 minutes.

In the meantime, drain beans and potatoes and blanch in boiling water. When water returns to a boil, drain and add to tomato mixture. Cover and simmer over medium heat for 15 to 20 minutes or until beans are tender. Add warm water if needed. Serves 6 to 8.

BROCCOLI CON OLIVE
Broccoli with Olives

1 bunch broccoli
2 cloves garlic, finely chopped
4 tablespoons olive oil
1 cup coarsely chopped tomatoes
1 cup pitted black dried olives
Salt and freshly ground black or hot pepper

Preheat oven to 400°. Cut large broccoli flowerets in half. Peel broccoli stems and cut in quarters or halves, depending on thickness. Soak broccoli in salted cold water for 30 minutes before cooking. Blanch broccoli in boiling water. When water returns to a boil, drain thoroughly.

Put garlic, olive oil and tomatoes in a medium-sized pan. Simmer, uncovered, for 3 to 4 minutes. Add broccoli, olives and salt and pepper to taste. Cover, and bake for 10 to 15 minutes. Do not overcook. Serves 6.

Note: This dish can also be cooked on top of the stove.

CAVOLI CON POMODORI E PATATE
Savoy Cabbage with Tomatoes and Potatoes

1 Savoy cabbage (1¾ to 2 pounds)*
2 cups potatoes, peeled and cubed
6 tablespoons olive oil
1 clove garlic
2 cups coarsely chopped tomato
1 tablespoon fresh sweet basil or 1 teaspoon dried basil
Salt and freshly ground black or hot pepper

Discard tough outer leaves of cabbage. Cut remaining cabbage into small pieces. Soak in cold water for ½ hour. Place potatoes in water with cabbage. Drain and blanch vegetables in pot of boiling water. When water returns to a boil, drain.

Meanwhile, place olive oil in a wide skillet. Sauté garlic in oil, and when it begins to brown, add tomatoes, sweet basil and pepper to taste. Simmer for 5 minutes.

Add cabbage and potatoes to tomato mixture. Add salt to taste and simmer over medium heat for about ½ hour or until cabbage is tender. Serves 6.

    * Ordinary cabbage can be used in this recipe, but it is not as tasty.

CAVOLFIORE CON ACETO E POMODORI
Cauliflower with Vinegar and Tomatoes

A head of cauliflower
6 tablespoons olive oil
1 cup chopped onion
3 tablespoons wine vinegar
1 cup coarsely chopped tomato
1 tablespoon dried sweet basil
Salt and freshly ground black pepper

Cut cauliflower into flowerets and blanch in salted boiling water. When water returns to a boil, remove cauliflower and drain.

Place cauliflower with olive oil in a skillet. Cook, uncovered, over moderate heat until edges of cauliflower begin to brown. Add onion, and when onion wilts, add vinegar and cover. Lower heat and cook for 3 to 4 minutes. Add tomato, basil and salt and pepper to taste. Cover and simmer until cauliflower is tender. Do not overcook. Serves 6.

MELANZANE ALLA PARMIGIANA
Eggplant Parmigiana

1 eggplant, about 1 pound
1 medium onion, chopped
¼ cup olive oil or half oil and half butter
1½ cups seeded and chopped tomato
½ cup water
1 teaspoon dried basil or 1 tablespoon chopped fresh basil
1 teaspoon chopped parsley, Italian if possible
1 teaspoon oregano
Salt and freshly ground black pepper
2 eggs
Grated Parmesan cheese
Flour
Corn oil or peanut oil
¾ cup cubed mozzarella cheese
2 slices prosciutto, chopped

Preheat oven to 400°. Cut eggplant into ⅛-inch slices and set aside.

Sauté onion in olive oil. When onion wilts, add tomato, water, basil, parsley, oregano and salt and pepper to taste. Simmer, uncovered, over low heat for 20 minutes, stirring occasionally.

Beat eggs with 2 tablespoons of the Parmesan cheese. Dip eggplant slices into egg mixture, then dust each slice with flour. Pour enough corn oil into a cast-iron skillet so it comes to about ¾ inch from the top of the skillet. Heat the oil to very hot. Check temperature by flicking flour into oil—when the oil boils violently, it is hot enough. Drop each slice of eggplant, one at a time, into the hot oil. Cook for 1 minute or until eggplant is lightly browned. Blot on paper towels and keep warm. Repeat process until all eggplant is cooked.

Pour some of the tomato mixture on the bottom of a casserole approximately 9 by 12 inches. Add layers of cooked eggplant, tomato mixture, grated Parmesan cheese, mozzarella and prosciutto. Repeat the process until all the eggplant is used, pouring extra sauce and cheese on top of the final layer of eggplant. Cover, and bake for 20 minutes. Let the dish stand for 10 minutes before serving. Serves 6 to 8.

Note: An excellent lunch.

MELANZANE RIPIENE ALLA SICILIANA
Stuffed Eggplant Sicilian Style

1 large eggplant
2 cups chopped tomato
¾ cup chopped onion
2 tablespoons olive oil
Salt and freshly ground black pepper
¼ pound ground lean chuck
¼ pound ground lean pork
¼ cup grated Parmesan cheese
¼ cup bread crumbs
1 tablespoon chopped parsley, Italian if possible
1 egg, lightly beaten
¾ teaspoon finely chopped garlic

First, make sauce. Strain tomatoes through a sieve. Brown onion in 1 tablespoon of the olive oil. When it begins to wilt, add tomato and salt and pepper to taste. Cover and cook over medium heat for 15 minutes.

Meanwhile, in a large bowl, mix chuck, pork, cheese, bread crumbs, parsley, garlic and salt and pepper to taste. Mix well and form into three meatballs, flattened so that they are about 1¼ inch thick.

Place remaining tablespoon of olive oil into a small skillet. Add the flattened meatballs and cook several minutes over low heat. As soon as meat changes color, turn each meatball with a spatula. Increase heat to medium, and brown meatballs, turning occasionally so they do not stick.

Preheat oven to 400°. Cut the eggplant crosswise into four equal slices. Place a browned meatball between the slices of eggplant to make one large sandwich, with eggplant at each end. Tie the sandwich together with heavy string.

Place the stuffed eggplant in a pan that holds it tightly. Pour prepared sauce over it, cover and bake for about 35 minutes, basting occasionally. Remove cover and sprinkle eggplant with additional cheese. Bake for several minutes under high heat to brown. Excellent with rice. Serves 4.

SCAROLE CON ACCIUGHE
Escarole with Anchovies

1 pound curly escarole
4 anchovy fillets
4 tablespoons olive oil
1 clove garlic, finely chopped
3 green olives, pitted and sliced *
Salt and hot red pepper

Clean and soak escarole in cold water for 30 minutes. Drain and chop coarsely. Drain anchovy fillets and cut into ½-inch pieces.

Cook escarole and garlic in olive oil, uncovered, over high heat for 7 minutes. Add olives, anchovy fillets and salt and pepper to taste. Cover pan and continue to cook over high heat, stirring occasionally, for 15 minutes or until escarole is tender. Serve hot to 4.

* Olives must be whole and packed in brine. Available in Italian and Greek food stores.

FINOCCHIO COTTO
Cooked Fennel

3 medium fennel bulbs
2 cloves garlic, minced
2 tablespoons butter
2 tablespoons olive oil
Salt and freshly ground black pepper
Grated Parmesan or Romano cheese

Cut fennel in slices, discarding hard core and tough outside leaves (save leaves for soup or pasta sauce).

Place all ingredients, except cheese, in a wide skillet. Cover, and cook over low heat for ½ hour or until fennel is tender. Serve with grated cheese to 4.

WILD MUSHROOMS

Anyone who has not tasted a fresh wild mushroom is missing a great gastronomic joy. And nothing is more exciting and sensual than to brush aside some leaves and find on the ground a great cluster of mushrooms with the fragrance of the earth.

In Italy large mounds of wild mushrooms fill the markets during spring, early summer and fall, and America also has a fantastic quantity and variety of wild mushrooms. I am not an expert and I will not attempt to describe them, but most Italians of my father's generation knew a great deal about wild mushrooms and loved to gather them. My father himself gathered a variety of five or eight wild mushrooms he recognized.

During the Depression we would walk about five miles to get to the fields and pastures where the mushrooms were. We would take huge sandwiches made of homemade bread, a bottle of my father's wine for us to drink and a bottle to give to the farmer to allow us to gather on his fields. My father carried a two-bushel basket and I carried a small one.

From September through November it was a joy to be in the woods. We would gather mushrooms until we filled our baskets and then walk back home with our baskets on our backs. My mother would wash the mushrooms, checking the ones I had picked with special care. Then she would can them several different ways. We had Mason jars full of mushrooms for meats and sauces all year long.

I remember one funny day when my father and I were gathering mushrooms in a pasture on a low hillside. I couldn't have been more than ten at the time. Suddenly in the distance I heard strange noises, the blowing of bugles, the thunder of hooves and shouts. We knew nothing of such strange sounds and we just ignored them and continued to pick some lovely boletus that grew there in abundance. The din grew louder and louder until the hunt was upon us. People dressed in red coats and white breeches and women in black hats and what looked like men's coats were leaping over us on their enormous horses. It seemed insane to me that the crowd of them were going in such haste to God knows where, their crazy dogs howling and running all over the place. I looked at my father for an answer. He looked at me, shrugged his shoulders, and said, "Well . . . ," meaning something like, There's no explaining the behavior of the insane of the world. We then continued to pick those mushrooms left untrampled by the passing madmen.

VERDURA TROVATA
(Found Vegetables)

My favorite vegetable dish is called *verdura trovata* (found vegetables). My aunt, Zia Pippina, used to prepare it for me on her farm in Italy. It is a dish most Italians never heard of. It is impossible to order it in a restaurant and impossible to buy the ingredients in a store. The only way to taste the dish is to be invited to an Italian farmhouse for dinner.

There you will be served a variety of about twenty wild vegetables and herbs and also cultivated vegetables that are gathered from the fields. It used to take my aunt half a day to find enough for eight people.

The vegetables are cut in small pieces—most are small leaves of herbs. Diced potatoes are added and everything is blanched, then drained and cooked in a cast-iron skillet with olive oil and garlic over a wood fire. The potatoes dissolve during the cooking and mix with the liquids from the vegetables to form a thick sauce. The taste is a delight to experience. We always had verdura trovata with rabbit.

I have tried to make something similar with the first spring vegetables and herbs that appear in my own garden —small cabbages that grow on old cabbage stalks, garlic greens, dandelion greens, rugola, turnip greens, etc. I have had excellent success with certain weeds I have found in my garden, such as wild spinach (also called lamb quarters or pigweed), redroot, purslane, wild asparagus and wild watercress. It is all very tasty but not like my aunt's. In fact, several vegetable dishes in this book are my creations, inspired by my verdura-trovata experience. They are my attempts to make a dish as good as Aunt Pippina's.

VERDURA MISTA #1
Mixed Vegetables (An Interpretation of Verdura Trovata) #1

1 large potato
1 stalk celery
½ pound escarole
1 pound fresh spinach
½ pound Savoy cabbage (ordinary cabbage will do)
3 tablespoons olive oil
2 cloves garlic, finely chopped
Salt and freshly ground black pepper

Peel and dice the potato. Clean celery and cut into 1-inch pieces. Wash and chop escarole, spinach and cabbage. In a deep pot, blanch all vegetables together. When water returns to a boil, drain and set vegetables aside, saving ½ cup of the liquid. Heat oil and garlic in a wide skillet. As garlic begins to brown, add vegetables and salt and pepper to taste. Cover, and cook over low heat until vegetables are tender. Add reserved water as needed. Serves 6 to 8.
Note: Some of the vegetables in this dish will blend together—this is what is supposed to happen.

VERDURA MISTA #2
Mixed Vegetables #2

1 small eggplant
2 zucchini
4 tablespoons olive oil
3 cups chopped, seeded tomatoes
2 green peppers, sliced
2 medium potatoes, sliced
2 tablespoons fresh basil or 1 tablespoon dried basil
2 medium onions, sliced
Salt and freshly ground black pepper to taste

Cut eggplant into 1-inch cubes and the zucchini into ½-inch slices, place in a wide skillet or pot with olive oil and heat. Add rest of ingredients. Partially cover skillet and cook, over medium heat, stirring occasionally, until potatoes are tender. Serves 6 to 8. *Note:* With a poached egg on top, this makes an excellent main course.

PISELLI CON UOVA
Green Peas with Eggs

¼ cup chopped pancetta or lean bacon
1 medium onion, chopped
3 cups green peas
2 cups stock or water
1 teaspoon basil
2 eggs, well beaten
Salt and freshly ground black pepper to taste

Sauté pancetta or bacon. When it is half cooked, and before it begins to brown, add onions. When onions wilt, add all remaining ingredients except eggs. Cover and cook gently until peas are tender. Then add eggs and mix well for several minutes. Turn off heat and allow to stand for several minutes. Serve hot as a vegetable to 6.
Note: Excellent with grated Parmesan or Romano cheese.

PISELLI AL PROSCIUTTO
Peas with Prosciutto

2 cups green peas
1 medium onion, chopped
2 tablespoons olive oil or half oil and half butter
½ cup chopped prosciutto
1 tablespoon chopped parsley, Italian if possible
Salt and freshly ground black pepper

Put peas in a small pot and cover with stock or water. Cook until tender. Drain.

In the meantime, sauté onion in oil in a small separate pot. When onion wilts, add prosciutto, parsley, salt and pepper to taste, and cook for 1 minute. Add to peas. Cover and simmer over low flame for 10 minutes. Serves 4.

Note: Fresh green peas should not have to be boiled first, but I have found that unless I use peas from my garden they almost always need pre-boiling.

PEPERONI IMBOTTITI
Stuffed Peppers

½ can (small) anchovies, chopped
3 tablespoons bread crumbs
½ teaspoon finely chopped garlic
1 tablespoon chopped parsley, Italian if possible
1 tablespoon grated cheese, Parmesan or Romano
1 egg, lightly beaten
5 tablespoons olive oil
Salt and freshly ground black pepper
3 large bell peppers
½ cup chopped tomato
¼ cup water
½ teaspoon oregano

Mix together well: anchovies, bread crumbs, garlic, parsley, grated cheese, egg, 3 tablespoons of the olive oil and salt and pepper to taste. Set aside.

Wash peppers. With a sharp knife cut a hole at end of each pepper and pull out core; reserve the cap end. Fill peppers with stuffing and put caps back on. Sauté peppers in the remaining 2 tablespoons of olive oil. When tender, set aside and keep warm.

Meanwhile, in a separate covered pot, combine tomato, water, oregano, salt and pepper to taste and cook over medium heat for 5 minutes. Stand peppers upright in a baking dish and pour sauce over them. Cover and simmer for 25 minutes. Serves 3 to 6.

PATATE CON OLIO DI OLIVA
Boiled Potatoes with Olive Oil

3 medium potatoes
3 teaspoons olive oil *
Salt and freshly ground black pepper

Boil potatoes with their skins on. When they are tender, remove skins and crush potatoes roughly with a fork. Add olive oil, salt and pepper to taste and toss lightly. Serve hot, with more olive oil if desired. Serves 3 to 6.

* It is essential that excellent olive oil be used. I prefer olive oil to butter on potatoes.

PATATE ALLA PARMIGIANA
Parmesan Potatoes

4 medium potatoes
Butter
3 tablespoons Parmesan cheese
4 tablespoons diced mozzarella cheese
2 tablespoons chopped parsley, Italian if possible
2 eggs, beaten
Salt and freshly ground black pepper to taste

Preheat oven to 400°.

Boil potatoes in their skins. When tender, remove skins and mash potatoes. Allow to cool to room temperature.

Butter a baking dish. Mix remaining ingredients with potatoes and spread mixture in dish so that it is about 2 inches thick. Bake in oven, uncovered, for 10 to 15 minutes or until potatoes brown. Serve hot to 6 to 8.

BROCCOLI DI RAPE
Rape

A broccoli-like and delicious green, used in both Chinese and Italian cooking. It is available in late fall and winter in specialty markets that deal in Italian or Chinese foods.

4 pounds fresh rape
1 cup olive oil
3 cloves garlic, finely minced
Pinch of hot crushed pepper (optional)
Salt to taste

Clean the rape by removing the large tough leaves. Cut the smaller tender leaves into 2-inch pieces, leaving the buds intact. If the stems are tender enough to eat, cut them in half lengthwise and cut into 2-inch pieces. Drop the rape into salted boiling water, and when the water returns to the boil, drain immediately. Save ½ cup of the cooking liquid. Place the rape in a saucepan with the oil, garlic and hot pepper. Do not add liquid but cover tightly. Cook the rape 15 to 20 minutes or until tender. Add a little of the reserved cooking liquid if the vegetable becomes too dry or starts to burn. Serves 6 to 8.

BROCCOLI DI RAPE CON FAGIOLI
Rape and White Beans

2 pounds fresh rape*
½ cup olive oil
2 cloves garlic, finely minced
Hot red-pepper flakes
1 can cannellini beans, drained **
Salt and freshly ground black pepper

* Savoy cabbage and escarole may be substituted for the rape, but they must be simmered until tender before combining with the beans.
** You can use 2 cups dried white beans, soaked overnight, and cooked in water until tender.

Clean rape according to directions on page 202. Cook in boiling water to cover for 2 minutes. Drain, but reserve ½ cup of the cooking liquid. Put the rape in a medium-sized skillet and add the oil, garlic, pepper and pepper flakes to taste. Add ½ cup of the cooking liquid and simmer 5 minutes. Add beans and salt to taste. Cover and simmer 15 minutes. Serves 6.

SPINACI CON PATATE
Potatoes with Spinach

2 pounds fresh spinach
1 large potato
2 cloves garlic, finely minced
¼ cup water
¼ cup olive oil
Salt and freshly ground black pepper

Wash the spinach well and discard any tough stems. Drain and set aside. Peel and thinly slice potato. In a large saucepan with a cover, place the potato slices, garlic and water. Cover and simmer until tender but not mushy. (The saucepan must be large enough to hold the spinach when it is added.)

Add the spinach, olive oil, salt and pepper to taste and simmer, uncovered, over high heat, turning constantly with a two-pronged fork. The cooking time should be no longer than 5 minutes and most of the liquid should evaporate. Serves 4 to 6.

SPINACI AL FORNO
Baked Spinach

This is an excellent recipe, difficult to match, but fresh spinach must be used. My first choice is fresh loose spinach. If not available, fresh packaged spinach can be used.

4 tablespoons olive oil or half oil and half butter
2 cloves garlic, finely chopped
2 pounds fresh spinach, well washed
Salt and freshly ground black pepper

Preheat oven to 400°. Pour olive oil in ovenproof casserole, add rest of ingredients, cover and place in oven. Stir occasionally. Spinach will be ready in 15 to 20 minutes. Do not overcook. Serves 4.

ABOUT TOMATOES

Since so many recipes in this book require tomatoes I thought the reader would like some information about preparing them for cooking.

There are a number of ways to prepare fresh tomatoes for sauce, but since I find many of them messy and not too efficient, I use my mother's way. If a recipe calls for an uncooked tomato, my mother just rubs the tomato with the blade of a knife (the tomato darkens as it is rubbed), rather than dropping it in boiling water or peeling it with a knife. She then pierces the skin with the knife point, and the tomato will peel almost as easily as when dropped in boiling water. You must then remove the seeds because they make your sauce bitter.

In salads, Italians, and especially Italian farmers, generally prefer half-green tomatoes to very ripe ones. For my own taste, I find that half-green tomatoes complement vinegar and lemon better. Then, too, half-green tomatoes have a lovely refreshing texture, while overripe tomatoes may be soggy.

In testing these recipes I used only garden-fresh tomatoes or home-canned organically grown tomatoes from my garden. Very sadly I have discovered that because Italians now also rely on artificial fertilizers and chemical insecticides, imported Italian tomatoes are no longer very good. This is a fairly recent change. As for American canned tomatoes, the less said about them the better. It is depressing to feel that we are slowly being poisoned to death by the food we eat. I canned a hundred quarts of tomatoes—organically grown tomatoes—in my garden last summer. I realize most people do not have the facilities to have a large garden, which is unfortunate because it seems to me it is becoming a question of survival. I think this is the reason young people are aware of this and are very interested in raising their own food.

ZUCCA CON POMODORI
Zucca with Tomatoes

3 cups zucca,* cut into 1-inch pieces
3 tablespoons olive oil
1 medium onion, sliced
2 tablespoons chopped parsley, Italian if possible
1 teaspoon dried basil or 1 tablespoon chopped fresh basil
½ cup chopped tomato
Salt and freshly ground black pepper to taste

* Zucca is available during the summer and fall in Italian stores. Some Italians call the zucca "cocozza." It is zucchini grown until it is about 12 inches long and 3 inches in diameter. The soft centers and seeds should be removed. The flesh is better in soups and stews than zucchini, which has a tendency to dissolve when cooked too long.

Scrub and remove soft centers and seeds from the zucca. Heat oil in medium-sized skillet. Add zucca and cook over high heat, turning often and carefully with a spatula. As zucca begins to brown, add onion. When onion wilts, add the remaining ingredients. Cover and lower heat. Simmer for about 15 minutes. Good hot or cold. Serves 6 to 8.

Note: Potatoes are excellent in this dish. Thinly slice about 2 medium potatoes and add them at the same time as the zucca.

FIORI DI ZUCCHINI
Zucchini Flowers

The flowers of zucchini plants are harvested during the summer months. The male flower grows on a long straight stem. The female flower, which appears simultaneously with a baby zucchini at the end, grows on a short stem off the stalk. If the female flower is not fertilized by pollen from the male, both the flower and zucchini drop off and die. Usually, there are many more male flowers than are needed on one plant and it is the male flowers which are harvested.

They are eaten in several different ways; the most popular is to dip them in batter and deep-fry them. Children love the idea of eating flowers.

Zucchini flowers are sometimes available in Italian markets during the summer months, though you will probably have to order them in advance. The flowers have an exquisite flavor. Any kind of squash or pumpkin flower is edible.

16 to 24 zucchini flowers (they should not be too limp)
2 eggs
1 tablespoon water
Salt and freshly ground black pepper
Flour
Corn or peanut oil

Check closed flowers for bugs and bees. Then wash them carefully so that they do not break.

Beat together eggs, water, salt and pepper to taste. Dip each flower in the egg batter, then dust with flour.

Pour enough oil into a cast-iron skillet so that it comes to within about ¾ inch of the top of the skillet. Heat oil until it is very hot. Test by flicking flour into the oil. If the oil boils violently, it is hot enough. Add the zucchini flowers, one at a time. Cook until golden brown, not *too* brown. The flowers will cook in about 1 minute. Remove each flower with a slotted spoon, drain on paper towels and keep warm. Repeat process until all flowers are cooked. Serve immediately, as a vegetable, to 4.

ZUCCHINI CON PATATE
Zucchini with Potatoes

2 cups zucchini, sliced into ½-inch pieces
3 tablespoons olive oil
1 medium onion, sliced
½ cup chopped tomato
2 medium potatoes, diced
1 teaspoon oregano
Salt and freshly ground black pepper to taste

Sauté zucchini in olive oil in uncovered skillet over high heat. Stir often (zucchini becomes soggy unless lightly browned first). As zucchini begins to brown, add remaining ingredients. Cover, lower heat and simmer until potatoes are tender, about 15 minutes. Serve hot or cold to 4.
Note: Excellent served with grated Parmesan cheese.

salse

Sauces

SALSA VERDE ALLA MARCHIGIANA
Green Sauce Marchigiana

1 cup bread crusts, finely chopped
3 tablespoons wine vinegar
1 tablespoon finely chopped fresh mint
3 tablespoons finely chopped parsley, Italian if possible
6 anchovy fillets, drained and finely chopped
4 tablespoons olive oil
Salt and freshly ground black pepper to taste

Soak bread crusts in vinegar. Mix together with remaining ingredients and blend well. Serve with boiled meat. Yields ¾ cup, or enough to serve 4.

SALSA GREMOLADA
Gremolada Sauce

½ cup finely chopped lemon peel
2 teaspoons finely chopped garlic
3 tablespoons finely chopped parsley, Italian if possible
2 tablespoons olive oil
Salt and freshly ground black pepper to taste

Mix together all ingredients and add to sauces or stews during the last 5 to 10 minutes of their cooking time. Yields about
¾ cup. Use with stews, especially Osso Bucco (page 151).

SUGO DI POLLO PER LA PASTA
Macaroni Sauce with Whole Chicken

A 3-pound chicken
¾ cup cubed salt pork
Giblets
1 onion, stuck with 4 cloves
1 whole garlic clove
½ cup dry white wine
4 cups fresh or canned tomatoes, peeled and strained
6 tablespoons tomato paste
¾ cup warm water
1 teaspoon chopped fresh or dried sweet basil
Salt and freshly ground black pepper
1 tablespoon butter

Soak the cleaned chicken in cold water to cover for 2 hours.
Put the salt pork into a deep kettle or Dutch oven and when it
starts to throw off fat, add the whole chicken. Turn the chicken
in the hot fat so that it browns evenly for about 5 minutes. Add
giblets, onion and garlic and continue turning the chicken on all
sides. Drain off and discard all but 3 tablespoons of fat. When

chicken is golden brown, add the wine. Cover, and cook over low heat about 10 minutes. Using a slotted spoon, remove the cubes of salt pork and discard.

Meanwhile, in a kettle large enough to hold the chicken, combine the tomatoes, tomato paste, warm water and blend. Cook 5 minutes. Add the chicken and juices in which it was browned. Add basil, butter and salt and pepper to taste. Cover partially and cook over low heat for 1½ hours. Serve the sauce first with any desired freshly cooked pasta, such as spaghetti or linguini. Serve the chicken as the main course to 4 to 6.

SALSA AL MARSALA
Marsala Sauce

½ cup dry Marsala, imported if possible
1 clove garlic, chopped
Salt and freshly ground black pepper
3 cups veal stock
1 tablespoon butter

Put wine in a skillet or pot with garlic and pepper to taste. Turn up heat and cook, uncovered, until reduced to ⅔ of its volume. Add veal stock and continue to reduce for 1 minute. Add salt to taste and put liquid through strainer. Remove from heat, add butter and blend well. Serve hot on veal or chicken. Yields about 2 cups.

SALSA MARINARA
Marinara Sauce

This recipe was given to me by a Florentine while we were living in Florence. It is the best marinara sauce I have ever tasted.

¼ cup olive oil
2 cups coarsely chopped onion
½ cup sliced carrot
2 cloves garlic, finely minced
4 cups canned Italian plum tomatoes
Salt and freshly ground black pepper
4 tablespoons butter
1 teaspoon dried oregano
1 tablespoon chopped fresh basil or 1 teaspoon dried basil

Heat the oil in a large open skillet and add the onion, carrot and garlic. Cook, stirring, until the vegetables are golden brown. Pour the tomatoes through a sieve, pushing the pulp through with a wooden spoon. Discard the seeds. Add the puréed tomatoes to the vegetables and add salt and pepper to taste. Partially cover and simmer 15 minutes. Put the sauce through a sieve and push the solids through with the wooden spoon. Return to the skillet and add the remaining ingredients. Partially cover and simmer 30 minutes longer. Yield: 3 to 4 cups.

VARIATIONS

With mushrooms: Quarter ¾ pound of fresh mushrooms and cook them in 2 tablespoons olive oil, plus 2 tablespoons butter, until golden brown. Add the mushrooms to the sauce for the last ½ hour of cooking.

With meatballs: Combine ½ pound twice-ground pork or veal with 1 egg, lightly beaten, ¼ cup chopped parsley, ½ cup bread crumbs, grated rind of ½ lemon, 2 tablespoons grated fresh Parmesan cheese, ¼ teaspoon grated nutmeg, and salt to taste. Add ½ garlic clove, finely minced, if desired. Shape the mixture into 12 small balls and dust them lightly with flour. Brown on all sides in 2 tablespoons oil, plus 2 tablespoons butter. Add the meatballs to the sauce for the last ½ hour of cooking.

With sausages: Broil 2 sweet or hot Italian sausages, turning occasionally, until done. Cut the sausages into ½-inch-thick slices. Add to the sauce for the last ½ hour of cooking.

SUGO DI CARNE
Meat Sauce

4 cups fresh or canned ripe tomatoes
½ cup olive oil or 1 cup cubed salt pork
1 pig's foot or 1 large pork chop*
1 shin of veal or shank of veal, if available
¾ pound chicken wings, necks or backs
1 beef soupbone
¾ pound chuck, preferably with bone
1 onion stuck with 4 cloves
2 whole garlic cloves
1 teaspoon whole crushed peppercorns or freshly ground pepper to taste
½ cup dry white wine
1 tablespoon dried fresh basil or 6 fresh basil leaves
1 can (6-ounce) tomato paste
Salt to taste
2 tablespoons butter

Heat the oil or render the salt pork in a large deep skillet or in a kettle and add the pig's foot, veal, chicken, beef bone and chuck. Cook, stirring with a wooden spoon, until meat starts to brown. Add the onion and garlic and continue cooking until meat is *thoroughly* browned. Add the peppercorns, wine and basil, and continue cooking until the wine evaporates. Set the kettle aside.

* Almost any bony pork parts, such as spareribs and neck bones, may be used with or instead of pig's feet and pork chops. Sweet Italian sausages may also be substituted.

If fresh tomatoes are used, core and peel them. Work fresh or canned tomatoes through a sieve or strainer to remove the seeds, which give a sauce a bitter taste. Bring the tomatoes gradually to a boil. Add the tomato paste and salt. Stir to blend and add to the meat and bones. Add the butter and partially cover. Simmer gently for 2 hours, stirring all around the bottom frequently, taking care that the sauce does not scorch or burn. (If it is not stirred, it will burn.) Yield: Enough for 2 pounds of pasta.

PESTO

Pesto is used as a sauce on pasta, on fish, and on meats. It is really good on everything. The sauce is a specialty of the Ligurian coast and the inland area in that part of Italy. The ingredients vary greatly, and every recipe is considered authentic by those who use it. I have a number of "authentic" pesto recipes, given to me by Genoese and other Italians. When I was in Genoa I tried to find the truly authentic version, but that experience convinced me that there is no such thing, just as there is no authentic minestrone or marinara sauce.

Several of my favorite pesto recipes follow here, but these are a very small selection from a vast number. The basic ingredient of pesto is fresh basil. I was told in Genoa that it is essential to make pesto with the small-leaf basil—a type I've never been able to find in America. I was also told that very little parsley must be used and that grated pecorino or Sardo is the best cheese. I myself have found that pignoli nuts give the pesto an excellent creamy taste, but I don't think that this would be as good on fish as the plain version.

Pesto takes some effort to make but it is well worth the trouble. It will not spoil if covered with about three quarters of an inch of olive oil. Then you can spoon out a little at a time as you need it. It will refrigerate or freeze, although I find the flavor best if it is just placed in a crock, covered with the oil and kept in a cool place. (Pesto with ricotta, of course, would have to be frozen.)

Pesto is a traditional sauce whose origin is Genoese. There are many versions of it, but the two characteristic ingredients are basil and garlic. The principal use is with freshly cooked pasta but it is also added at the last minute to soups, such as minestrone, and to almost any meat, fish or tomato sauce.

PESTO #1

The original way to make pesto is with a mortar and pestle. The solids and the olive oil are added slowly as the pesto is worked. The result is a looser pesto with a rougher texture.

5 cups fresh basil leaves, washed, drained, and tightly packed
¼ cup chopped parsley, Italian if possible
¾ cup olive oil
2 tablespoons finely minced garlic
½ cup pignoli nuts
1 teaspoon salt
½ cup pecorino or Parmesan cheese (I prefer pecorino)

Add all the ingredients to the container of an electric blender and blend, stirring down with a rubber spatula as necessary, until a smooth paste forms. Unless the pesto is to be used immediately, spoon it into a Mason jar or plastic container and cover with about ¾ inch of olive oil. Cover tightly and store in the refrigerator or in a cool place.

It may be kept indefinitely and used at any time, spooned directly from the jar onto pasta or into a sauce. Use about ½ cup pesto or less, diluted with about 2 tablespoons of warm water, for each pound of freshly cooked pasta. Toss quickly and serve immediately on hot plates. Yield: 2 cups of pesto.

The following pesto recipes are prepared, stored and served in the same way as Pesto #1.

PESTO #2

2 cups chopped fresh basil
3 tablespoons olive oil
3 tablespoons chopped lemon rind
3 tablespoons chopped parsley, Italian if possible
1 teaspoon salt
Freshly ground black pepper to taste

Yield: About ¾ cup. Excellent on spaghetti or linguini.

PESTO #3

2 cups coarsely chopped fresh basil
1 tablespoon chopped parsley, Italian if possible
1 tablespoon chopped garlic
¼ cup olive oil
6 chopped anchovy fillets
Salt and freshly ground black pepper to taste

Yield: About ¾ cup, or enough for about 1 pound macaroni. Excellent on spaghetti, linguini or spaghettini.

PESTO CON RICOTTA
Pesto with Ricotta

4 cups fresh basil leaves, washed, drained and tightly packed
4 tablespoons finely chopped parsley, Italian if possible
⅓ cup olive oil
1 tablespoon salt
2 cups drained ricotta
⅓ cup grated Sardo or Parmesan cheese

Yield: About 4 cups. Serve on any pasta with grated Parmesan or Sardo cheese.
Note: This recipe is quite mild.

SALSA PER POLENTA
Sauce for Polenta

*This sauce was usually made on my grandfather's farm
with very ripe fresh tomatoes.*

¼ cup salt pork or pancetta, chopped with a heated knife
½ pound fresh Italian sausage
1 medium onion, chopped
10 ounces dried mushrooms or ½ cup sliced fresh mushrooms
2½ cups tomatoes, strained
1 teaspoon basil
Salt and freshly ground black pepper
Polenta
Grated Parmesan or pecorino cheese

Heat salt pork. As it dissolves, add sausage and brown, uncovered, over moderate heat. Turn occasionally. When sausage
is brown, remove salt pork and discard. Add onion and cook
until wilted. Set aside and keep warm.
In the meantime, if dried mushrooms are used, soak in warm

water for 15 minutes. In a separate pot, cook tomatoes for several minutes. Slice sausage into ¼-inch pieces and add with fat to tomatoes. Add mushrooms, basil, salt and pepper to taste and simmer, partially covered, over low heat for about 45 minutes.

Pour cooked polenta, ½ inch thick, on each heated plate. Pour sauce, including mushrooms and sausage, over each plate of polenta. Serve with a generous amount of grated Parmesan or pecorino cheese. Serves 6.

Note: To make polenta, boil 1 quart water with 2 teaspoons salt. Add 1 cup finely ground yellow corn meal and stir constantly, cooking over medium flame for about 20 minutes.

SALSA RAGÙ
Ragout Sauce

1 slice salt pork, about 4 inches long by ½ inch thick
¼ pound lean ground beef
¼ pound lean ground pork
1 small onion stuck with 3 cloves
1 whole garlic clove
Salt and freshly ground black pepper
½ pound (about 2 cups) mushrooms, sliced
½ cup dry white wine
1 teaspoon dried basil
4 cups tomatoes, strained
2 tablespoons tomato paste
½ cup warm water
1 tablespoon butter

Sauté salt pork. When it browns, remove and discard. Put ground meats, onion and garlic in the pot. Cook, uncovered, over moderate heat, stirring often with a wooden spoon. Add salt and pepper to taste. When meat begins to brown, add mushrooms and continue to cook for several minutes, then add wine and basil. Cover and lower heat. Simmer for 5 or 6 minutes. Dilute tomato paste in warm water. Remove cover and cook out rest of wine. When wine cooks out, add tomatoes, tomato paste, butter, salt and pepper to taste. Simmer over low heat, partially covered, for 1 hour. Yield: Enough sauce for 1½ pounds macaroni.

TOMATO SAUCE

In making a pasta sauce with tomatoes there are a few important facts to remember. First of all, it is important to remember that the longer the sauce cooks, the more bitter and acid the sauce becomes. The idea of simmering a sauce for hours on end, which some people think makes it authentic, is wrong and a great way to have heartburn for dessert. During my six years in Italy or in my mother's house I never saw an Italian cook a tomato sauce for more than two hours.

The sweetest sauces are marinara sauces. In these, the tomatoes never cook for more than one hour and, more often, for no more than forty-five minutes. The least bitter sauce I have ever tasted is the marinara sauce on page 214 and it takes only about thirty minutes.

A minimum of tomato paste should be used, unless, as in Italy, homemade tomato paste is used (even then, it is used in small quantities). In a meat sauce, it is the bones, not the meat, that enrich the sauce. In Italy my relatives used to make a marvelous sauce with a beef bone, some pork bones and the feet, neck and head of a chicken. Bones such as veal bones, pork bones and chicken bones are excellent for a meat sauce. It is the gelatin in the bones that sweetens the sauce. Another important factor to remember is that the meat and bones should be cooked until they are very brown before the wine and tomatoes are added. If you feel the sauce is still bitter, use carrots instead of sugar. Butter will also mellow the sauce.

SALSA BESCIAMELLA
White Sauce

THIN SAUCE

1 tablespoon butter
1 tablespoon flour
1 cup milk
Salt and freshly ground black pepper to taste
Dash of nutmeg

MEDIUM SAUCE

2 tablespoons butter
2 tablespoons flour
1 cup milk
Salt and freshly ground black pepper to taste
Dash of nutmeg

THICK SAUCE

3 tablespoons butter
3 tablespoons flour
1 cup milk
Salt and freshly ground black pepper to taste
Dash of nutmeg

Heat butter, and as soon as butter melts, add flour. Stir with wire whisk until blended.

In a separate pot, bring milk to a boil. Add milk to flour and butter, stirring rapidly with a whisk until blended. Stir frequently and cook over low heat for about 15 minutes. Yield: 1 cup.

SALSA DI NOCI
Walnut Sauce

This sauce is excellent on fettuccine, cappelletti and ravioli.

½ cup shelled walnuts
¼ cup pignoli nuts
½ teaspoon marjoram
3 tablespoons olive oil
½ cup ricotta (optional)
Dash of nutmeg
Salt and freshly ground black pepper to taste
½ cup heavy cream

In a wooden bowl, mash walnuts and pignoli until they have a grainy consistency. Add all remaining ingredients except cream. (Sauce may be prepared ahead of time to this point.)

Add cream to sauce just before draining pasta. Yield: About 2 cups.

PANE, PIZZE
E DOLCI

Breads, Pizza
and Desserts

About

Breads

I have lumped breads and pizzas together with desserts because I cook so few desserts and have not been exposed to them much in my life.

In my own family and in Italy in general, desserts are made only on special holidays—though then they appear in great abundance. At home we would have fresh fruit when it was available or, occasionally, a sweet bread or a simple biscotti. Now, however, my own children will eat as many desserts as Ellie will make for them. I try to discourage this in our house, to get them to eat fresh fruit. I would like it if they too thought of desserts as very special foods, linked with traditions. It seems to me very unhealthy to have that much sweets as daily fare.

Several years ago my mother taught my wife, Ellie, how to make bread. However, the lessons didn't come to much until last winter when we had a very severe snowstorm in Katonah, New York, where we live. It was so severe that we were snowed in for five days. Rather than a traumatic experience, that week turned out to be a delight for all of us. We ate our own fresh and good frozen and canned garden vegetables, the tuna we had canned, etc. Ellie decided to get out my mother's recipes and to try to bake bread. Her effort was a wonderful success and she has been at it ever since. We no longer buy bread at all.

PANE
Bread

5 cups unbleached flour*
1 teaspoon salt
1½ teaspoons dry yeast
2 cups warm water

Mix all ingredients in a bowl. Add more water if too dry, and knead until well blended. Flour a board, and knead and roll dough, adding more flour if needed.

Put dough in a bowl, cover and allow to rise to double its bulk. Punch down, knead it again, cover and allow the dough to rise to twice its size a second time.

Preheat oven to 450°.

Place dough in 2 small floured bread pans. Bake for 25 minutes, or until a golden brown. Then lower to 350° and bake for another 45 minutes until crust is a deep brown. Yield: 2 small loaves.

> * Unbleached flour is available in most stores. It makes a better bread and is healthier for you.

PANE ALLA NONNA GIOBBI
Grandmother Giobbi's Bread

5 cups unbleached flour*
1½ teaspoons dry yeast
1 tablespoon salt
1½ tablespoons corn oil
2 cups warm water

Put flour in a bowl and make a well in the center. Add yeast, salt and corn oil. Mix well, then add warm water and work and knead until velvety smooth.

> * Unbleached flour is available in most stores. It makes a better bread and is healthier for you.

Place dough in a clean bowl, cover with cloth and put in a warm spot. Allow to rise to double its size, then punch down and knead for 5 minutes. Return to bowl, cover with cloth and allow to rise to double its size a second time. Punch the dough down and knead for 5 minutes. Shape dough into 2 loaves, place dough in 2 floured pans, cover with cloth and allow to rise again to double its bulk. (Unlike my mother, I allow the dough to rise only twice and it works out well.)

Preheat oven to 450°. Bake bread for 25 minutes or until brown. Reduce heat to 350°, take bread out of bread pan and bake on rack in oven for 45 minutes. Yield: 2 small loaves or 1 large loaf.

PANETTONE ALLA MILANESE
Christmas Bread Milanese Style

2 packages dry yeast
½ cup tepid milk
¾ cup sugar
6 eggs
1 teaspoon salt
1 pound butter, melted
6 cups flour
½ cup white raisins
½ cup chopped citron
2 tablespoons grated lemon rind

In a medium bowl, soften yeast in milk. Add sugar and mix well. Break eggs into bowl, one at a time, stirring as you add them. Add salt and melted butter. Mix well. Then add flour slowly, stirring constantly. Remove dough from bowl and knead on a floured board for 10 minutes. Put dough in a clean bowl and set aside in a warm place. Cover with a cloth and allow dough to rise until double its size.

Preheat oven to 350°.

After dough rises, knead in raisins, citron and lemon rind. Knead for about 15 minutes until it is the consistency of bread dough. Add more flour if necessary. Butter a round cake pan about 4 inches deep and 10 inches in diameter. Dust it with flour and place dough in pan. Bake 30 to 40 minutes or until crust is golden brown.

PIZZA CON BROCCOLI E TONNO
Pizza with Broccoli and Tuna

DOUGH

3 cups flour
3 tablespoons olive oil
1 teaspoon salt
1 teaspoon dry yeast
1 cup tepid water

FILLING

1½ bunches fresh broccoli
¾ cup olive oil
1 can (7-ounce) tuna, packed in olive oil
1 clove garlic, minced
Salt and freshly ground black pepper

Preheat oven to 400°.

Pour flour on a board and make a well in the center. Add olive oil, salt, yeast and water. Add water as you mix. Knead dough well. It should be consistency of pie crust. Cut the ball of dough in half and roll into two balls.

Clean the broccoli. Cut the flowerets in bite-size pieces. Peel the stems, quarter and cut into 2-inch lengths. Cook in boiling water for 4 minutes. Drain and put in a bowl with olive oil, tuna, garlic and salt and pepper to taste. Set mixture aside.

Roll out each ball of dough. Rub olive oil on the bottom of a baking sheet (15 by 10 by 1 inch). Place one piece of dough on the sheet, overlapping the sides of the sheet. Put in filling and place the second piece of dough over filling. Seal the edges by pressing them together. Lightly rub olive oil on the top. Bake for 15 minutes, then lower heat to 350° and bake 30 more minutes or until crust is golden. Serve hot or at room temperature to 6 to 8.

PIZZA CACCIA NANZA

The literal translation of caccia nanza *is "take out before." When bread was made in traditional Italian households, a bit of dough was reserved to make a pizza. The pizza was placed in the oven with the bread and obviously cooked more quickly. It was "taken out before" the bread, hence the name. Caccia Nanza is a specialty of Castel di Lama in the Marches. This is the only garlic bread I have ever eaten in Italy.*

2½ cups flour
½ teaspoon salt
¾ teaspoon dry yeast
1 cup lukewarm water
2 cloves garlic, thinly sliced
2 tablespoons rosemary
3 tablespoons olive oil
Salt and freshly ground black pepper to taste

Preheat oven to 400°.

Combine the flour, salt, yeast and water in a mixing bowl. Blend well, then turn dough onto a lightly floured board. Knead well, about 15 minutes, and shape the dough into a ball. Place it in a lightly greased mixing bowl. Cover with a towel and let rise in a warm place until double its size, about 1 or 1½ hours.

Turn the dough onto the board and knead once more. Put it back in the bowl and let rise again. Then punch down dough and turn it onto a lightly floured board. Roll it out to ½-inch thickness. Rub the surface of a baking sheet with oil. Transfer the round of dough to a baking sheet. Make indentations over the surface of the dough and insert a thin sliver of garlic and a bit of rosemary in each indentation. Pour the olive oil over the pizza and rub gently with the hands. Sprinkle with salt and pepper and bake 15 minutes or until golden brown. Remove the garlic before serving. Serves 4 to 6.

PIZZE FRITTE ALLA NAPOLITANA
Fried Pizzas Neapolitan Style

About ½ bread dough on page 228
1 cup chopped tomato
1 tablespoon olive oil
1 clove garlic, minced
1 tablespoon minced parsley, Italian if possible
½ teaspoon oregano
Salt and freshly ground black pepper
Corn or peanut oil
Grated Parmesan cheese

In a small skillet heat tomatoes, olive oil, garlic, parsley, oregano and salt and pepper to taste. Cover and simmer for 15 minutes, set aside. After dough has been allowed to rise twice, according to instructions, form pizzas by breaking off a piece of dough 2 inches square. With hands, form into rounds about 4 inches in diameter and ¼ inch thick. You should get 4 pizzas from the dough.

Heat oil in a skillet just large enough to hold 1 pizza. When the oil is very hot, add a pizza. Turn over to brown lightly on both sides. Blot on paper towels and set aside, keeping pizzas warm until all are cooked. Put a pizza in each plate, pour sauce over pizzas and sprinkle with a generous amount of grated cheese. Serve hot to 4.

Note: Use the same recipe for other types of pizze fritte: instead of tomato sauce, sprinkle with sugar or spread with honey or jam for breakfast. We always had pizze fritte for breakfast when my mother made bread.

PIZZA CON PROSCIUTTO
Pizza with Prosciutto

This pizza is a traditional Easter dish in many parts of Italy.

FILLING

½ pound prosciutto, in a slice ¼ inch thick
1 link dried Italian sweet sausage*
½ pound mozzarella, diced
1½ pounds ricotta
1 cup grated pecorino cheese

DOUGH

2 cups flour
2 eggs
3 tablespoons milk
2 tablespoons melted butter

* Imported from Abruzzi, if possible.

Preheat oven to 350°.

Dice prosciutto and sausage and then mix together with mozzarella, ricotta and grated cheese. Set aside.

Make a well in the flour and add eggs, milk and butter. Mix gradually and knead well. Roll mixture into a ball, cut the ball in half and roll out one half on a floured board to the thickness of pie crust. Lift into a 10-inch pie pan or baking dish and cover with filling. Roll out the remaining half of dough and then cover filling. Seal the edges by pressing bottom dough to top dough.

Bake for about 1 hour or until pizza is brown. Serve at room temperature to 6.

PIZZA CON CICOLI
Pizza with Pork

2 cups lean pork butt, cut into ½-inch cubes
1 cup lukewarm water
1 teaspoon dry yeast
3 cups flour
1 teaspoon salt
10 crushed peppercorns
½ cup grated Parmesan cheese or half Parmesan and half pecorino
Butter

Cook the pork in a greaseless skillet until brown. Drain off and reserve the fat. Use the fat to rub the bottom and sides of a bread pan about 10 inches in diameter. Reserve the meat and let it cool.

Combine ¼ cup of the water with the yeast and let stand briefly. Sift the flour into a mixing bowl and add the yeast, the remaining lukewarm water, salt, peppercorns, cheese and pork pieces. Knead the mixture until it holds together, then turn it out onto a flat, lightly floured surface. Knead about 100 strokes, 2 minutes or longer. Shape the dough into an oval and place it in the greased bread pan. Rub the top with butter and cover with a cloth. Let it rise in a warm place until double its size in bulk, about 1½ hours. Punch down dough and let it rise again.

Preheat the oven to 450°. Bake the dough 30 minutes and reduce the temperature to 350°. Bake until surface is brown, about 20 minutes longer. Yield: 1 pizza loaf.

PIZZA CON RISO #1
Pizza with Rice #1

This is another traditional Easter dessert in many areas in Italy, especially in the mountain regions where sheep are raised.

FILLING

½ cup rice
1½ cups milk
1½ pounds ricotta
½ cup sugar
1 grated lemon rind
¼ teaspoon cinnamon
3 eggs

DOUGH

2 cups flour
2 eggs
2 tablespoons sugar
3 tablespoons melted butter
½ grated lemon rind
½ teaspoon baking powder

Preheat oven to 400°.

Cook rice in milk until tender. Cool and add to other filling ingredients. Mix together well and set aside.

Put flour on a board. Make a well in the center and add remaining dough ingredients. Knead into a smooth mixture. Add warm water to dough, if needed. Roll out like pastry, saving enough dough to make 6 strips 1 inch wide across the width of pie plate. Line bottom and sides of a 10-inch pie plate with dough. Put in filling and lay the strips over filling in a criss-cross pattern. Place in oven and after ½ hour lower heat to 350°. Bake another 30 minutes. Cool before serving. Serves 6 to 8.

PIZZA CON RISO #2
Pizza with Rice #2

This is also a traditional dessert we had every Easter in my mother's house.

FILLING

½ cup rice
2 cups milk
3 eggs
1 grated lemon rind

DOUGH

1 cup flour
2 tablespoons melted butter
1 tablespoon sugar
½ teaspoon baking powder
1 egg

Preheat oven to 350°.

Cook rice in milk until tender. Cool. Then mix with eggs and lemon rind. Set aside.

Put flour on a board. Make a well in the center and add the butter, sugar, baking powder and egg. Mix together and knead well. Roll out as you would pastry and line bottom and sides of a 10-inch pie plate. Add filling and bake for about 1 hour. Serve at room temperature, although it is also excellent straight from the refrigerator. Serves 6 to 8.

TORTA DI MANDORLE
Almond Cake

A traditional Christmas cake common in the areas of Italy where almond trees grow.

¼ pound butter, melted and cooled
1 cup sugar
1 teaspoon vanilla
2½ cups flour
2 tablespoons grated lemon rind
¾ cup milk
3 teaspoons baking powder

Mix butter and sugar together. Add vanilla and mix well. Then add flour and lemon rind and mix again. Add milk and baking powder, stir together thoroughly and set batter aside.

FROSTING

1¼ cups almonds
2 egg whites
1 teaspoon vanilla
1 cup sugar
2 tablespoons grated lemon rind

Preheat oven to 400°.

Boil almonds for 1 minute in water, drain and remove skins. Place almonds on a baking sheet and toast them in oven until lightly browned. Be careful not to burn them. Shake occasionally. Finely chop almonds by hand or put them in a blender.

Turn down oven to 350°. Mix egg whites and vanilla together. Then add sugar, almonds and lemon rind and mix well. Butter a baking pan (13 by 9 by 2½ inches) and lightly flour it. Pour batter into pan. Spread frosting over the batter and bake 40 minutes or until golden brown.

BISCOTTI CON MANDORLE
Biscuits with Almonds

1 cup almonds
4 cups flour
4 eggs
1½ tablespoons grated lemon rind
5 tablespoons butter, melted
4 teaspoons baking powder
5 tablespoons sugar, plus small amount to sprinkle on top
1 egg yolk, beaten

Preheat oven to 400°.

If fresh almonds are used, shell them. Boil them for 1 minute in water, drain quickly and remove the brown skins. Place on a baking dish and bake until toasted. Do not burn. Then finely chop almonds by hand or in a blender. Place the flour in a mixing bowl and make a well in the center. Break the eggs into the well, add the almonds, lemon rind, butter, baking powder and the 5 table-spoons of sugar. Blend well.

Divide the dough into five pieces. Roll each piece on a lightly floured board to ½-inch thickness, about 2 inches wide and 10 inches long. Continue until all the dough is rolled out. Brush the tops of the rolled-out strips with egg yolk. Sprinkle with sugar and bake 20 minutes or until top is golden. Cut the strips while hot at an angle to make biscuits about ¾ inch wide. Yield: About 50 biscuits.

CALGIONETTI

This pastry has a provincial honesty that is a delight. It is a Christmas specialty from the Marches and was always my favorite. My mother made calgionetti only during the Christmas holidays and they were made two different ways. The first was with grape concentrate (set aside when we made wine in the fall), mixed with bits of chocolate and almonds. The other way was with chick peas (ceci beans) and honey.

FILLING

¾ cup shelled almonds
1½ cups canned or dried chick peas, soaked overnight and cooked until tender
2 tablespoons grated orange rind
¼ teaspoon cinnamon
4 tablespoons honey

DOUGH

3 cups flour
½ cup dry white wine
½ cup water
½ cup olive oil
Pinch of salt

Put almonds in boiling water. Boil for about 1 minute or less, drain and remove brown skins. Place in tray and put in 400° oven, mixing occasionally. Remove when brown, cool and finely chop. Set aside.

Drain chick peas and put through mill or sieve. Add almonds, orange rind, cinnamon, and honey. Mix well and set aside.

Make a well in the flour. Put other ingredients in well. With a fork gradually work in flour until mixture thickens. Then continue mixing with hands. Knead dough until well blended. Roll into a ball, then cut in half and make 2 balls. Flour a board, roll out one ball with rolling pin to a circle about $\frac{1}{16}$ inch thick. About 2 inches from the top of the circle put 1 teaspoon of filling every 2 inches across the width. Roll 2-inch strip over top. Seal bottom edge. With sharp knife or pastry wheel, cut out individual calgionetti in half circles as you would ravioli. Seal edges with a fork and set aside. Repeat process until all of the circle is used. Then roll out other half of dough and repeat process.

In a skillet put about 1 inch of corn oil or peanut oil. When oil is very hot add 5 or 6 calgionetti, one at a time, and deep-fry until they are golden brown on both sides. Remove from oil, blot with paper towels and repeat process. Sprinkle sugar over calgionetti when finished. Yield: About 60 calgionetti.

PESCHE IN VINO
Peaches in Wine

This was a favorite of my father's. It has the honesty and simplicity of the Italian contadino.

Fresh peaches
Dry red wine

Fill a wine glass with slices of peeled ripe peaches. Pour dry red wine over the slices. Eat the peaches with a fork and drink the wine afterward.

Excellent too with dry white wine and, for those who can afford it, champagne.

PALLINE DI RICOTTA
Ricotta Balls

3 eggs
2 tablespoons sugar
1 pound ricotta
1 cup flour
5 teaspoons baking powder
¼ teaspoon salt
2 teaspoons brandy
Corn or peanut oil
Powdered sugar

Mix all ingredients together except oil and powdered sugar. Cover and let rest for 1 hour. Put about 1½ to 2 inches of oil in a small skillet. Heat the oil until it is quite hot. Then drop 1 teaspoon of batter at a time into skillet (the oil should boil violently when batter is added).

Cook 5 to 6 minutes or until balls are golden brown. Remove with a slotted spoon, blot on paper towels and dust with powdered sugar. Serve warm. Yield: About 48 balls.

INDEX

About the Author

EDWARD GIOBBI lives in Katonah, New York, with his wife and three children. He grows his own food, makes his own wine, raises rabbits, chicken and ducks, and produces huge and beautiful canvases which appear in some of the most notable private collections in the country as well as in several museums.